Grassroots Christianity

Grassroots Christianity

The Church As It Was Created to Be

Duncan Kellard

Authentic

HYDERABAD · COLORADO SPRINGS · LONDON

Grassroots Christianity
by Duncan Kellard

Copyright © 2008 by Duncan Kellard

First edition 2008
Revised edition 2009
ISBN: 978-81-7362-843-6

Published by Authentic Books

P. O. Box 2190, Secunderabad 500 003, Andhra Pradesh.
www.authenticindia.in

9 Holdom Avenue, Bletchley, Milton Keynes, MK1 1QR, UK
www.authenticmedia.co.uk

1820 Jet Stream Drive, Colorado Springs, CO 80921, USA.
www.authenticbooks.com

Scripture quotations used in this work are taken from the *King James Version* (KJV), *New International Version* (NIV) of the Bible.

Authentic Books is an imprint of Authentic India, the publishing division of Biblica South Asia.

Contents

Acknowledgments

To my wife, Sara, for your uncompromising desire to find God's best. Thank you for joining me on this uncharted adventure, and for your love, encouragement, wisdom, tears and laughter.

To Pat and Jenny Kellard, my parents, whose God-filled, unconventional and radical lives have taught me to seek the life of God and resist the lure of "success" as defined in our time.

To Josh and Katie, my children, the most precious gifts entrusted to us, what a privilege! Thank you both for being you and blessing others by displaying God's gifts so naturally.

To Stour Valley Community Church who have encouraged (and sometimes endured!) my leadership these many years, for your partnership, adaptability and trust. Most of all thank you for being a wonderful family to us.

To mentors, many and varied, including Phil Dowding (my youth leader), Mike Frisby and Ken Matthews (firebrands, apostles and friends), for teaching me to follow the Spirit.

To my fellow leaders down the years including Gary Fry (for your friendship), Mike Haine (for your humor and care), Neil

Croucher (for your honesty and help) and Ian Smith (for giving me courage, and for staying the course!)

To the "ordinary" saints (a contradiction in terms) who have proved that God delights to use the weak, for teaching me that my prime responsibility as a leader is to encourage and release your gifts for kingdom work.

Most of all to my God, who is the only God, Father, Son and Holy Spirit, for loving me, having mercy on me, giving me everything I do not deserve, and for using someone so weak and fallible.

Introduction

The church that changes the world. . .will not look impressive. It will not possess great buildings, nor its leaders hold high social standing. It will shun wealth and political acceptance, and run shy from the world of brands, image and sound bite.

The world-changing church, will be powerful in the things that matter, a simple dependence on the power of the gospel, the inspiration of the Holy Spirit and the authority of God's Word; a people who love their God, love each other, and live salty lives as Christ's disciples thus provoking both conversion and persecution.

It might be hard to find (in terms of buildings, services and projects), but impossible to escape. It will be meeting in your street and your workplace.

This book offers a provocative challenge to institutional Christianity, a way ahead for those tired of mere human organization, and hope to those who long to see the Spirit of God springing up and blade by blade, transforming the nations.

This book has been written by someone who loves the church and delights to find the needle of vitality amongst the haystack of human trappings! The purpose in these writings is not to convince, but to provoke; provoke thought, reflection and action.

It is to challenge the deadening trend towards "humanizing" the work of God in his church, and to inspire believers in whatever setting to move along the continuum towards a more flexible, simple reliance on the Holy Spirit in church life.

Whilst the author has numerous friendships with Christians from many denominations, and has worked in association with several groups (notably New Frontiers and the Evangelical Alliance), it should be noted that the views expressed herein are his alone (at present!).

The author also willingly acknowledges that his own contribution to the work of the kingdom is miniscule in comparison to countless saints who work in far more institutionalized settings.

Yet it is written with a conviction that the work of Restoration, which has been visibly revolutionizing the church since 1517, is entering a new epoch; a time when the church will, at last, shed its institutional guise and be seen purely for what it is, the Spirit-filled, God-loving, gospel-preaching people of God.

Then will the world, once more be "turned upside-down" (that is to say, "right side up!").

Duncan Kellard,
Palawan, Philippines.
March 2008.

Prologue

Life Springs Up

It seemed to have started by accident: This group, this "church," this gathering in homes.

When the Greens moved to Hazleford, a village in rural Wiltshire, they did what they always tried to make time for after their evening meal, (when there was nothing else pressing). They read a verse or two from the Bible, talked about how it applied to their lives, prayed a bit and sang some praise songs. It was simple but real, and everyone took part. It might last a few minutes after a tiring day, sometimes half an hour or more if a meaty discussion or lively praise time developed. The washing-up could wait!

When Jackie (the Mum) invited their recently widowed neighbor Lily for a meal one Tuesday, she couldn't imagine what she had started. After eating they had their usual "devotional"—normal for them, but life changing for Lily. A "church" attendee all her life, she had never prayed aloud before and never discussed the Bible. Yet she loved it, and soon her visits became almost weekly and within two months God had moved, in her experience, from a distant figure of reverence to being her loving heavenly Father.

Tuesday seemed to be the best evening for these "open suppers," and Lily's new found enthusiasm and the fact that she knew almost everyone in Hazleford meant that visitors were often coming "for a look," some just the once, others becoming regulars.

Mark, the Dad, seemed to have a gift for explaining the Bible when questions came up, Jackie was a great hostess, inviting people freely and putting them at their ease. The children—Phil (fourteen) and Rosie (twelve) mixed well with all ages and very naturally used their spiritual gifts; Phil being quite prophetic, and Rosie compassionate and helpful to anyone who was sad, lonely or shy.

In time, numbers swelled to a regular fifteen. People arrived 5.30–6.00 p.m. for a meal (which became by necessity quite simple), and with most people contributing food, the work and cost were shared. Over those meals friendships were forged across the false divides of age, education and "class." Troubles were shared, solutions discovered and laughter brought its unique healing touch. As in any family, for that was how it felt, squabbles and differences arose.

But these were overcome and, in a funny way, the group became closer as a result of being able to be real, facing and overcoming their conflicts and learning to set aside their own preferences.

After the clearing up, around 7.00 p.m., they would sit back down for a meal of another kind. Like the food it was simple and different every week. Single mum Tina might share a story of how God had provided for her that week. This might inspire Tony (a fifty-year-old plumber) to read a Psalm. Songs and prayers and spiritual gifts would flow (often from the half-dozen kids and young people present). Needs were shared, advice from the Bible given, prayers were lifted. It could have been chaotic, but it seemed there was an unseen conductor uniting this disparate "band" into a beautiful, unplannable harmony. By 8.00 p.m. or so some of the younger families had to be getting children to bed and so another precious evening drew to a close.

One year later the group reminisced about the highlights. Was it the day that Tony's wife Jean had finally plucked up courage to come and ended up becoming a Christian within weeks? Or perhaps it was that April evening when three of the group received the Holy Spirit and spoke in tongues? Tina's announcement of her engagement to Jack had produced tears of joy too. And the July evening when half a dozen had been baptized in a pool in the back garden was unforgettable. God had done so much. Little of it had been foreseen, none of it planned, at least not by a human mind. . . .

Thoughts turned to the future. The group now numbered twenty, half from Hazleford, and the rest drawn from neighboring villages.

Jack had a bright idea. "Why don't we start a proper church?"

Jean chipped in, "We could hire the village hall—no one uses it on Sunday mornings."

Lily spoke up, "Good idea, they have that room at the back which would be perfect for a Sunday school."

The conversation picked up momentum, "Of course we'd need a Pastor." No one disputed this.

"Why not ask Mark. If we all gave a bit, we could pay him part time until we grew enough to afford more."

They turned to Mark, who had been quiet for quite sometime. He looked strangely wistful; some thought they saw his eyes glisten with tears. What was he thinking?. . .

To be continued—In the Epilogue. . . .

1

A Life of Its own
The Grassroots Understanding

A minister was asked to look after another church for a few weeks at very short notice. He began his first talk "As I have had no opportunity to prepare for today, I shall have to speak only the words which God puts in my mouth"; before adding "Next week I shall prepare something much better!"

Oh Man!

It was Groucho Marx who claimed to have sent a telegram to his club: "Please accept my resignation. I don't want to belong to any club that would accept me as a member."

It puts me in mind of my Dad's wise (if slightly mischievous) advice to restless people who rarely settled in a church for very long before moving. "There's no such thing as the perfect church" he would say. Then, after a pause and a smile to soften the impact, he'd add, "but if you do happen to find one, don't spoil it by joining!"

The fact is that this amazing body of people we call "the church" is a blend of all God's wonderful, powerful perfections, alongside every manner of human failing and folly.

At the heart of this book is the conviction that the church—in Scripture, in History and today is at its best when human intellect and organization defers to God's unfathomable wisdom, and when our confidence is placed fully in his strength and leading, not man's.

The Two Thousand Year War

For two millennia a battle has raged for the soul of the church. And still the conflict rages. It is the contest between:

The life of God, as he moves unpredictably and powerfully saving and transforming lives and creating Spirit-filled communities, and. . .

The desire of man, to own, control and contain the work of God through traditions, programs and human authority structures.

Inspiration versus Institution

The church was born, and has flourished, in adversity. The fledgling community received rejection from the Jews then repudiation by the Romans. They had no buildings, no social standing, no trained leaders, little education and no clever game plan or "vision" (the sacred cow of the modern church). No plan, that is, apart from the Great Commission (Matt. 28:19–21).

But they had the life of God! The Gospel—which they preached in all its offensive, glorious power provoking either conversion or persecution. The Spirit—who caused them to love as they had never loved before, and perform miracles and signs that gave credibility to their revolutionary message; and the Word of God—their mandate and guide and the authority they depended upon.

Far from protecting this vulnerable newborn, the Lord permitted it to be scattered in a wave of opposition that took the lives of beloved leaders like Stephen and James. Sounds like a death-blow? Yes, but "those who were scattered by the persecution in connection with

Stephen traveled as far as Phoenicia, Cyprus and Antioch telling the message. . .to Jews."[1] Others then, (horror of horrors!) preached to the Greeks. And we read on "The Lord's hand was with them, and a great number of people believed and turned to the Lord."[2]

God was not prepared for his precious bride to become acceptable and institutionalized (or mono-ethnic) in a world system that—at its root is in enmity to the kingdom of God. Yet in being rejected, it thrived as believers bereft of human influence depended fully on God's power both to deliver them and make their message fruitful.

As long as the church functioned in this way, stewards rather than owners of the Gospel and deposit of truth, then it flourished. The moment forces of religiousness, tradition and human control were insinuated, life began to be quenched.

Lessons from History

The two thousand year history of the church can be interpreted in many ways. For an increasing number of modern commentators a clear pattern has emerged:
• God breaks out in power.
• Real worship, spiritual power and many disciples result.
• Forces of traditionalism and human control creep in
• Spiritual impact becomes diluted, and the raw edge is blunted
• God breaks out somewhere new!

There was an almost inevitable tendency for the "official" church to look upon any new outbreaks as heretical, especially as these exhibited a spiritual power and experience alien to the increasingly atrophied establishment. Tragically, in marginalizing such "charismatic" groups, the established church made them vulnerable to error thus causing their contribution to be further discredited.

So whether we consider the second century Montanists, the pre-Reformation Hussites, Lollards and Waldensians, eighteenth century Moravians or present-day Chinese Underground Church, we see repeatedly, fresh power injected into eras of spiritual decline. These movements themselves often "aged" into traditionalism (or were crushed by the outraged establishment they challenged). So a phenomenon emerges, that can be summed up thus—Inspiration releases life, Institutionalism eventually quenches it.[3]

Because the tendency of any significant movement is to become institutionalized, the best, longest standing examples of simple, inspirational church life occurs where either persecution or poverty prevent the church from becoming more "sophisticated," and the raw, rustic state is maintained and multiplied.

The Chinese Example

In the post Soviet world, the best current example is the Chinese Underground Church. Numbering in excess of hundred million believers they own no buildings, employ few staff (although thousands of young "evangelists" are sent with minimal funding to take the gospel to new regions), and enjoy no social acceptance, having nothing to motivate them, but God's glory and the saving of the lost.

I was privileged in 2002 to visit a number of Chinese "house" churches in three geographically and socially disparate locations. The same qualities were evident. Simplicity (worship, prayer, teaching, evangelism and fellowship were the only agenda); Passion (unrestrained joy, affection, tears and wholehearted devotion), and Participation (there was in no way a leader / people divide and the ubiquitous term "coworker" conveyed the palpable sense of body ministry).

Is organization wrong? Surely we should do things well?

It is often argued, usually from Acts 6 when the apostles "organize"

food distribution to widows in Jerusalem, that human organiz
a helpful thing that makes the church more efficient. The content
of this book is that while yes, any group of people—even a small
family—needs a degree of organization, that should not be what
defines it. Certainly not the church!

The early church was minimalist in organization, they
emphasized living the life. Today's church is normally content if the
"organization" works (the building gets looked after, the services run
smoothly, the books balance and the program gets out on time), even
if such "success" conceals an absence of salvation or discipleship or
supernatural activity.

What would happen if the buildings were taken away, the
services canceled and the "ministers" and "staff" removed from
office? If congregations, unable to go to "church," formed themselves
into small, local groups meeting "leaderless" in their homes? If the
structure and trappings were removed, would anything survive?

A Recent Striking Example

In 1982 a Soviet backed communist coup took place in Ethiopia.
Churches were "closed," their meetings banned, their buildings
confiscated and their senior leaders imprisoned.

At that time the Mesorite Church in the capital (Addis
Ababa) numbered five thousand members. Overnight it vanished.
Unaware of each other, many tiny local groups began to gather
inconspicuously in homes for fellowship, worship and discipleship.
In time, some leaders who had remained free gave themselves to
distributing "equipping" materials, fragments of teaching, to aid the
ministry of these secret small groups.

No public evangelism was permitted, but the believers found
they could "get away with" unrestrained gospel preaching at funerals
and so new people were saved through public as well as private

...embers felt they were merely preserving a
...rough a time of persecution.
... years later, the Communist government
...re released, church buildings were returned
...eting was possible. Imagine their joy and
...hat their church had not only survived, but
had grown tenfold to number fifty thousand people![4]

Today's western church is organizationally defined

The church, in any biblical sense, cannot be described as an organization. It can be only properly defined in terms of spiritual life, relationships and purpose. Yet say "church" today to the proverbial "person-in-the-street" and they will understand you to mean a building or, possibly, a weekly Sunday service.

But to someone in first century Palestine or Asia Minor, it meant something far less mundane and more substantial! A distinct community who exhibited true spiritual power, with a radical message ("Repent! Turn around!"). They ate together, worshiped together, were prepared to make enormous sacrifices and yet worked hard in "ordinary" ways and were well thought of in their localities. Their philosophy was simple and fivefold: Become more like Jesus, worship God by the Spirit, pass on the gospel, lovingly share lives together and let all members play their part.

How then might we rediscover the raw, life-changing power of the early church? To begin with, we will need to be willing to jettison much that has attached itself to this "living organism" over two thousand years of institutionalization. How we love our buildings, our full-time staff, our state of the art communication skills and our slickly run services and programs.

How proud we are of our worship band (or choirs), worship leaders and power-point presentations. They speak of "excellence" and give us "credibility" (so we imagine) in a hi-tech world. How we depend on our highly organized church calendar with its comforting predictability, structured teaching program and appealing literature and publicity.

The premise of this book is that far from helping us attain the life of the early church, the trappings of organization and institutionalism often hinder it and more alarmingly cloak a loss of vital purpose. People are preached to but wouldn't choose to be called "disciples," they experience high quality music, but often struggle to engage in worship, they fund expensive missions but may lack the boldness or desire to share the gospel with friends or colleagues.

The good news—life is waiting to break out!

Have you ever noticed (especially in your driveway or on your patio) how wild flowers and grass force their way through concrete and pavements? The great news is that God's life too will always break through "spiritual concrete." His purposes are never thwarted, his glory and victory assured. The big question is, how can we be agents of his life, rather than those who frustrate or dilute it?

What does inspirational church life look like?

What does a forest look like? What does a river look like? The point is that life is unique, every snowflake different and every human being distinct. So is every church that is born of God.

There is an amusing line at the beginning of a Fawlty Towers episode as a rare happy client pays and departs. Basil looks after him wistfully, "A satisfied customer, we should have him stuffed!"[5]

Sadly, for many of us in church life, especially leaders, we are often looking for what "works" elsewhere so we can distil it, bottle it or stuff it, and import this new technique, system or program into our church. I, along with many of my fellow leaders, spent years employing the different methods and systems that come along each year or so, and like some ecclesiastical Mr. Toad have jumped in glee saying "it's the only thing" until of course, the promised results don't quite materialize, and the next "thing" comes along.

For those looking for a new church "system" or "program" or "technique" this book will be a disappointment. It offers nothing so banal as a "how to guide" on more efficient church life. In fact it is the opposite. It is a (willing) admission, that the church is God's, the power is his and the plan is his. Our place is to live in the flow of that life, rather than trying to turn God's living river into a reservoir for our own convenience or reputation.

However, we can observe trends that betray a move from a church's (usually) inspirational roots to increasingly institutional outcomes. The rest of this book is devoted to discussing, in a practical way, how we (in whatever shape of church we currently belong) can resist the forces of human institutionalism, and move increasingly towards an abandoned dependence upon God's life.

A little of our story

Some years ago I became "burnt out." Trying to meet others' expectations, trying to prove myself, even trying to justify my salary, I saw the church I had "tried to build" start to unravel. No horrible split, just God moving half of the people on. I went into depression, tried to close the church (God didn't let that happen). So we just met. I "led" in a very low-key way, and we canceled all meetings but Sunday. But God turned up, sometimes very gently, sometimes powerfully. Worship happened. People opened their lives. An unsaved partner was drawn in and an unchurched Christian added. We found that what we strived to achieve in complex and exhausting ways, God began to do as we just met in his presence.

Contrasts between human sophisticated church forms and God inspired "grassroots" Christianity:

Institutional	Inspirational
Human organized	God inspired Ephesians 1:22–23.
Program dependent	Spirit dependent Ephesians 5:18–20.
Complex and structural	Simple and organic Ephesians 4:15–16.
Front led meetings	Everyone ministers 1 Corinthians 12:7.
Predictable	Powerfully unpredictable 1 Corinthians 14:26.
Cloned style and behavior	Great variety & character 1 Corinthians 12:4–6.
Professional clergy, passive body	Body works, "lay" leaders equip and release Ephesians 4:11–12.
Impersonal lecture teaching	Life applied & flexible Matthew 28:19–20.
Attendance orientated	Salvation orientated Acts 5:13–14.
Demanding schedule	Part of our daily life Acts 2:42–44.
"School" approach to children	Intergenerational life Matthew 14:21.
Formal, superficial relationships	Brothers and sisters Romans 12:9–10.
"Sanctuary" based	Home is central Romans 16:5, 23.
Seeks public acceptance and visibility	Grassroots impact Acts 2:46–47.

The grassroots quotient: "Our dependence on God is inversely proportional to the value we set on human method and ability."

Understanding Our Spiritual Genes

You don't have to tell grass to grow, a cat to purr or a hen to lay eggs. It's in their genes. Likewise in the spiritual "genes" of a Christian is a desire for all the things that church is about—a joy in worshiping God, a need to be more like Jesus, a wish that others might know him, a desire to join with fellow believers and a yearning to "be of use." Throw a bunch of Christians together anywhere and leave them to it and these five features will emerge.

So much of church activity is inspired by the erroneous assumption that unless a program is created, a powerful leader recognized, a spiritual secret discovered, or a brilliant method employed, that Christians will remain aimless, helpless, ignorant and useless!

The truth is very simple that, as with all of life, put any living thing in a suitable environment and it will become what it is created to be. In the case of the Christian, or the church community, that environment is simply to gather with mutual respect, honor God's Word and allow his Spirit to lead. The irony is that superfluous activities and the control inherent in institutionalism inhibit believers being what they were made to be. Their energy is sapped, gifts are frustrated, passion becomes dulled and their purpose fudged.

Why the nations need inspirational churches

Nearly every Christian must have quoted Zechariah 4:6, *"Not by might, not by power, but by my Spirit', says the LORD Almighty."* These words have been imbued with profound depth for me in recent years. I had paid them lip service whilst still trusting in my supposed might, power, and "good ideas." In (I hope finally) admitting the bankruptcy of mere human effort, I am discovering the riches of seeing what God will do when we slip across to the passenger seat.

This is not simply a matter of preferred style. Times of shaking have begun, not only in the church, but in the nation and world community too. For the church to be the effective instrument of kingdom advance we long for, there needs to be a wholesale loosening of grip on the external trappings, and a clinging on to God. "The people who do know their God will stand and do exploits!"[6]

Let's look at some of the areas where rediscovering a raw, rustic approach will release fresh power and joy into the church, both for its own health and also for the healing of the nations.

References

[1]Acts 11:19.

[2]Acts 11:21.

[3]A helpful study of the many "charismatic" movements through the ages can be found in John Wimber's 1984 study *Signs and Wonders and Church Growth* (Vineyard Ministries International).

[4]The video account of this astounding story entitled "Against all odds" can be obtained through the Mennonite Centre in London at www.menno.org.uk

[5]BBC Television 1975, Written by John Cleese and Connie Booth.

[6]Daniel 11:32 (King James Version).

_2_

There's No Place Like Home

The Grassroots Location

A mother and her young son entered the church service.
He chattered noisily and Mum said, "Quiet, this is God's
house." The boy looked around at the dark, stone-clad edifice
and said at last, "Well if I were God I'd move!"

Laughter, Love and Life

"These evenings have changed my life" said Tim, a thirty-eight-year-old policeman. "I'd like to get baptized."

The scene was our living room on a chilly February evening, sitting round a glowing log fire with mugs of coffee warming our hands. Tim was one of four unchurched friends who had been coming for a meal and to discuss Christianity for the past eight weeks. Jason, a thirty-year-old welder and biker, was equally enthusiastic, "I really want to get to know God and prove that he's real."

For two months they had met with six people from our church. Three of us had concentrated on cooking and serving and three had taken it in turns to give a short interactive talk, punctuated by intense discussion, personal sharing and vigorous laughter.

Steve, a mechanic in his mid forties, the quietest member of the group, seemed wholly at home and on the rare occasions he spoke, a growing appreciation of God's love was evident.

The last visitor was Ian, a real "life-and soul" character aged fifty who seemed to make everyone relax, regaling us all with outrageous anecdotes over supper. By his own admission a "cynical immigration officer," who had come mainly in order to understand his Christian wife, Ian found what he heard compelling. Within weeks he declared his belief in God, although it was two years before he turned that belief into a personal faith and commitment.

Would you like to come to church?

This was our fifth home-based outreach course, and a clear pattern was emerging. With one exception these courses resulted in clear conversions. Not only that but in only a few weeks deep friendships had been forged, and people had experienced first hand the power of God through answered prayers, a spiritual experience or healing.

As each twelve-week session drew to a close, the same sentiments were expressed; "Can we keep this group going, we have enjoyed it so much." On each occasion the encouragement to "come along on a Sunday" was given along with an invitation to "cell group" (Tim, the copper, never quite got his head around that!)

Yet the transfer rate, despite much prayer and offers of hospitality, proved poor. Out of a dozen genuine converts, only three eventually joined "the church," the others only visiting once or twice on Sunday, or failing to fit into an established home group. They did not "fall away" due to sin or unbelief, just the difficulty of connecting with a larger, more formal setting, having so enjoyed finding God and friendship in the home.

The home was central to the early church

When you read Paul's words *To the church of God in Corinth?* [1]

where do you envisage the letter arriving? In a church building perhaps? Or a big meeting with hundreds of people on benches facing the "front"? As church buildings were unheard of for two hundred years, it was almost certainly read to a bunch of believers squashed into someone's home, or sitting out in their courtyard.

The Greek word for "church" (ecclesia), simply meant "gathering" and was used in contemporary language to describe gatherings of many kinds.[2] Paul was as comfortable using it to describe the gathering of the city-wide church in Corinth as he was the church that met at Aquila and Priscilla's house (1 Corinthians 16:19).

The word "church" has acquired many theological barnacles and technical qualifications, but the inescapable fact is biblical usage simply communicates believers gathering as the body of Christ, whether locally in homes or in larger settings where, presumably, a number of local home churches would congregate.

The references to church in homes are plentiful enough to assert that a blend of local, smaller home meetings and a larger, probably less frequent, assembly across a region or city was the natural pattern. Consider the following examples:

"They broke bread in their homes and ate together with glad and sincere hearts" (Acts 2:46).

"Greet Priscilla and Aquila. . .also the church that meets in their home" (Rom. 16:3, 5).

"Gaius, whose hospitality I and the whole church here enjoy, sends you his greetings" (Rom. 16:23).

"Give my greetings to. . .Nympha and the church in her house (Col. 4:15).

". . .to Archippus our fellow soldier and to the church that meets in your home" (Philemon 2:1).

Additionally, as Michael Green points out,[3] particular homes were used by Paul as his base from which to evangelize and in which to gather and disciple:

Jason's house in Thessalonica (Acts 17:5).

Philip's house in Caesarea (Acts 21:8).

Titius Justus's house (provocatively next door to the synogogue!) in Corinth (Acts 18:7).

Lydia's home in Philippi (Acts 16 : 15) and, of course. . .

. . .Mark's Mum's "Upper room," the birthplace and earliest meeting place of the church (Acts 2 : 1,12:12).

Understanding the place of the home in church life

The New Testament churches did not have any buildings of their own—none, that is, except their homes. For more than two hundred years they thrived and spread using their homes, and occasionally a public meeting area, the Temple Courts in Acts 2 for example, or a public building, like the Hall of Tyrannus in Acts 19.

As the church became institutionalized, a ritualized Old Testament approach to church life was adopted with the introduction of altars, priests and "holy buildings." The spontaneity and family ethos of the church gave way to ritual, hierarchical control and the separation of "religious life," which happened in a "sanctuary," and "ordinary life" which took place in the home and workplace.

It can be argued that the style and practice of the modern church, whether traditional denomination or new charismatic, owes more to the institutional pattern than the raw, early church. In traditional churches, there may be "home groups" for the keen ones in the mid-week, but real church is perceived as what happens on Sunday. New churches, ironically, usually burst into life spontaneously in homes. But when they outgrow them, rather than starting new local home meetings, they move into a hall or school and the intimacy, participation and flexibility begin to wane immediately.

Yet it is almost impossible to create an environment for biblical church life when it takes place primarily in a central building and home church life is absent or merely a minority occupation.

In the home we eat together and forge the deepest friendships.

In the home everyone participates.

In the home people open their lives to one another and disciple each other through example and advice.

In the home Spirit-led flexibility takes place with ease.

In the home we relate with unsaved family, friends and neighbors.

We are a generation of institutionalized Christians

It is said that many children who grew up in the old style "children's homes" became institutionalized as adults, because a disciplined regime replaced the personal love of a family. Observers comment that having missed out on bonding with parents and siblings, such adults often tended only to thrive in a similarly "institutional" setting (such as the armed forces).

Sadly there is a parallel in the style of church where most of us were brought up or saved into. It was an organization more than a family. There was a dress code, a disciplined format of activities, a building laid out like a school classroom and a formal and reserved mode of relating to one another. For many of us there was a painful lack of some of the qualities we associate with a family: Genuine affection, individual nurturing, loyal devotion to one another, the ability to make a unique contribution, and the freedom to be ourselves as we laugh and cry and fail and win and grow.

Without devaluing what we may have gained from these settings, insightful teaching perhaps, moments of inspired worship maybe, even the time we responded to the gospel, should we accept our experience as the norm? Or dare we look again at Scripture and ask if what we have encountered in church life may be sub biblical?

Howard Snyder in his groundbreaking book, *Radical Renewal —The Problem of Wineskins Today* [4] addresses this issue candidly: "Whatever else church buildings are good for, they are not essential either for numerical growth or spiritual depth. The early church possessed both these qualities and the church's greatest period of vitality and growth was during the first two centuries when it did not have the help or hindrance of church buildings."

Snyder goes on to assert that church buildings, far from serving the purpose of advancing the kingdom, are actually "A witness to our immobility—our inflexibility—our lack of fellowship—our pride and—our divisions of class and race." Challenging stuff!

So what does the home have to do with this? What model does the New Testament offer? Should we revert to a less formal, home based format with all its chaos and smallness? Is that really church? Let's look at the one in whose steps we follow. . .

Jesus' ministry was largely home based

Jesus loved homes and loved eating with people. Flicking through Mark's Gospel we find Jesus:

• Healing Peter's mother-in-law at the family residence (1:29).
• Healing a paralytic via a hole in some poor soul's roof (2:10).
• Saving a bunch of crooked tax collectors at Levi's place (2:15).
• Getting mobbed and nearly "certified" over a meal (3:20).
• Healing a twelve-year-old girl in her bedroom (5:42).
• Telling the disciples to do home–based evangelism (6:10).
• Having his lunch interrupted by accusing Pharisees (7:2).
• Delivering a Greek girl from demons in a home in Tyre (7:24).
• Teaching the disciples humility in a Capernaum house (9:32).
• Giving revolutionary teaching on marriage in a home (10:10).
• Preparing for his last week at Lazarus' villa in Bethany (11:1).
• Being anointed by a sinful woman at Simon's dwelling (14:3).
• Instituting breaking of bread in a Jerusalem home (14:14).
• Enjoying a post resurrection meal at a disciple's place (16:12).
• Reuniting with the eleven in their locked-up home (16:14).
• Returning at last to his Father's house (16:19).

There were no barriers to Jesus' ministry

Church buildings today tend to lock Christians away from meaningful contact with their communities. Far from promoting the faith by being "visible" they mark the places for unbelievers to avoid! (Try inviting one in!)

For Jesus, his ministry seems to be about 40 percent in homes, 40 percent in informal gatherings in the open country or city courtyards, and maybe 20 percent in synagogues. Rather than being a model for the early church, synagogues were the hub of corrupt practice where Jesus confronted the religious establishment with true spiritual vitality. In Mark again we find Jesus:

• Upsetting the service expelling demons from a member (1:26).
• Chasing more demons from the Galilean synagogues (1:39).
• Having a contract put out on him for a Sabbath healing (3:1).
• Surviving a death attempt in Nazareth (6:2, see also Luke).
• Condemning the pride inherent in synagogue worship (12:39).
• Warning disciples they would be flogged in synagogues (13:9).

The synagogue therefore should not be seen as the forerunner of church life. This fact should at least bring into question our love of special buildings, formal seating, organized meetings and even the sacrosanct regular Sunday (or "Sabbath") meeting.

There is actually more resonance between the first church and early Jewish worship patterns which, unlike the synagogue, were divinely instituted. The weekly pattern was worship around the Sabbath meal with the extended household. Then seven times a year they would celebrate special feasts and seasons as a whole community. The regular meeting was small, home based and intimate.

Some reasons why homes are central to New Testament church life

Sincerity: Or put more simply "what you see is what you get!" Jesus' biggest beef with religious people was that they were "hypocrites," a word meaning "actors." It's not difficult to keep up appearances in public, but at home everything is on display. Whether we're kind or bad tempered, hard working or lazy, prayerful or profane, generous or covetous, the truth will out! Sound scary? Yes, when we have been used to worrying what people would think if they really knew what we're like! But don't worry; they're thinking exactly the same thing and its such a relief when we can all stop pretending.

Friendship: One of the biggest indictments of institutional church life, whether denominational or "charismatic" is the amount of people who feel they have no true friends. The whole front-led, large group style (even when the numbers might be modest), and the frigidity which public buildings provoke in all but the most gregarious, cause many to attend and leave without connecting with another person. The following is sadly the experience of many,

"I go to church each Sunday, and have done for many years.
(It's recently refurbished and has crystal chandeliers).
I hurry from the car park, a minute to half past,
And slip into the back row to find the first hymn fast.

I look around the gathering, familiar strangers all,
I know each name, and face (and hat!), like pictures on a wall.
But I don't know the joy or pain behind their Sunday smile.
And they don't know me either, (if they did they'd run a mile!)

I stand and sing, and sit and listen, hanging on each word,
Sometimes looking holy, and sometimes rather stirred,
But I long to shout out questions, and I long to say "Hey wait!
We're supposed to be a family sharing joy and grief and fate."

It's communion this morning, ushers pass along the pews,
With solemn, measured movements (have they automated shoes?)
If the trainer of the synchronized aerobics team were here,
He'd have them in the squad for the Olympic Games next year!

And now the service closes with the organ's harsh bellow,
As if to say "leave quickly before someone says hello";
Then a brief perfunctory handshake, 20 seconds at the door,
My total sum of contact then I'm in the car once more.

I go to church each Sunday, one hour spent to find
A surreal close encounter of a quite unearthly kind.
At home I read my Bible and think "there must be more
I want friendship, help and love, isn't that what church is for?"

How different when people meet in a home! Hosts bustling about getting tea and coffee, the murmur of half a dozen conversations, the interest expressed in pictures, books, musical instruments and the usual paraphernalia of family life. This ease transfers into the worship and teaching, as most feel free to contribute, discuss and ask questions, after all, it's not a service!

Discipleship: When you taught your kids to tie their shoelaces did you give them a half hour lecture and leave them to work it out? No you squeezed beside them on the third step of the stairs and got them to copy you! People do what they see us doing, rather than what we say they should do. Paul was able to say repeatedly "imitate me." He could only say this because people really knew him—not by attending his seminars, but because he lived and exercised his ministry in and around peoples' homes. Loving attitudes are observed and copied, problems are visible and can be gently taught into. It helps explain why hospitality is a non-negotiable qualification for church leadership in Scriptures.[5]

Mission: When the gospel is unfettered it can spread like an Australian bush fire, the wind of the Spirit making it jump as it were from tree to tree. Buildings take years to fund and years to build and immediately set a geographical limit on the impact of a church's ministry. How unlike both the early church and today's Chinese House Church!

Brother Yun, in his astounding account of the Chinese Underground Church[6] contends: "God has not only refined us in the fire of affliction for the past thirty years, He has also refined our methods. For example, we're totally committed to planting groups of local believers who meet in homes. We have no desire to build a church building anywhere! This allows the gospel to spread rapidly, is harder for the authorities to detect, and allow us to channel resources directly into gospel ministry."

Stewardship: In a related point, we need to question how much of kingdom money is eaten up by church building and maintenance. The physical needs of the worldwide church are immense, as is the need to fund mission to unreached people groups. Yet the scandalous fact is 90 percent of Christian money is spent on the world's richest 10 percent (USA, Western Europe and Australasia). This money is split between buildings and staff. Our nearest Cathedral costs £3,000.00 per day to upkeep or 1.1 million per year! That's enough to fund three hundred medics or teachers in Asia. What's the best value?

The recent trend for charismatic churches to build their own edifices perpetuates the problem. Less than thirty years old, many new churches have tired of the inconvenience of setting up in hired halls. A fellowship near us in Southern England raised 1 million to purchase a building five years ago (enough to build ten well equipped primary health centers in Africa) and have now announced a 1.3 million pounds refurbishment project (enough to fund a thousand Chinese evangelists for a whole year). What's more important?

Brother Yun again, "When I am in the West I see all the mighty church buildings and all the expensive equipment, plush carpets and state-of-the-art sound systems. I can assure the western church with absolute certainty that you don't need any more church buildings. Church buildings will never bring the revival you seek."[7]

Locality: How many people really belong to their local church? Most seem to drive at least a few miles, many ten miles or more. Their chances of getting a neighbor to come along is very slim, and the feasibility of fellowship between meetings is questionable, purely in terms of distance.

Imagine if we could forget our denominational tags for a moment and seek out Christians in our neighborhoods. Imagine those groups meeting regularly and committing to serve and reach the people they live among. Imagine groups like these meeting with others for a monthly celebration, for envisioning, teaching and encouragement. It may be a pipe dream, but it's a trend worth encouraging surely, and more reminiscent of New Testament method than the remote central church model we're stuck with now.

Participation: There are two dynamics here. First, people speak up in home gatherings in a way they are reticent to in the more formal setting of a hall. Second, quite simply the more people in a meeting the fewer will actively take part. The New Testament pattern describes an environment where "everybody has" a contribution (1 Corinthians 14 : 26). It is necessary therefore that there is a regular small home church gathering for this to happen. To be considered high priority it must take the place of the weekly Sunday service sometimes, rather than be an "optional extra."

Theology: Solomon wrote, *"The heavens, even the highest heavens cannot contain you. How much less this temple I have built!"* [8] Yet for a time, God chose to set his presence in a physical place. But when Jesus died the temple curtain was violently ripped into two. The temple is now replaced by groups of believers *being built together to become a dwelling in which God lives by his Spirit.* [9] The Bible could not be clearer, *"The Lord of heaven and earth. . .does not live in temples built by hands."* [10] Instead as Peter explains *you, like living stones, are being built into a spiritual house.* [11]

One of the most dominant New Testament pictures used to describe the church is that of a "household," God's household. Scriptural language is replete with the language of family, "brothers . . .sisters. . .mothers. . .fathers. . .devotion. . .love. . .help. . .care. . . eating. . . ." It figures that the most natural setting for this "household" is—you've guessed it—a house! And it was easy to see how the sense of family, and sharing of life and discipleship by example happened naturally in this most informal of environments.

Eating: Food is central to normal church life, because it is central to family life. The genius of Alpha is not the teaching (fine as it is there are many other courses equally good). . .it's the food! It's the Bible's pattern too: If you cut out all the accounts involving food in the Bible you wouldn't have much left! As enjoyable as big shared meals are with a large group in a hall, they are a lot of work and therefore only undertaken occasionally, if at all. But groups in homes can eat every time they meet. Breaking bread is transformed from being a solemn ceremony back to what Jesus modeled it to be—a beautiful reminder of his presence when we meet to eat together.

Welcoming newcomers: There is a perceived problem here. Some people feel that newcomers would be loath to visit a meeting in a house. Our experience has shown that, as long as a person has been befriended beforehand, they will quickly feel relaxed in a home meeting. There is no ceremony to observe and regulars are very welcoming. One of my church leader friends, an out-and-out evangelist, despairs when new people are often not spoken to when they visit his Sunday meetings in a school hall. Yet in a home people act differently and naturally chat to everyone in the room.

Some Common Objections

Over the past few years when I mention that we are a largely home based church, I have met with a few common objections from Christians belonging to "proper churches." In summary they are: "How does anyone know where you meet so they can come?" **Answer:** We invite friends and neighbors and word quickly gets round the area. We touch more lives than when "centralized."

"Don't people think you're part of some weird cult?" **Answer:** Most people think all Christians are a bit weird! The difference is that those we live among have got to know us as people, and judge us on the basis of what we are really like rather than according to a stereotype.

"It's so small! How can you have any impact?" This question is so important that it is dealt with in detail in chapter 6 ("Small Is Beautiful, Big Is Necessary." The clue is in the name of the book!

"We have home groups in the week but meet centrally on Sunday, we've got the best of both worlds!" It's true that the churches which are most successful (at evangelism, community and discipleship) are those who develop their small groups most effectively. We must realize though that they are the exception and very few churches have more than 30 percent of their members regularly attending a small group. Running the "Sunday show" each week takes enormous effort and time whether in an owned or hired facility. The balance of large and small meetings in the church will always favor the large, if the large event is always the weekly Sunday meeting.

How does a home meeting differ from a larger gathering?
It's 10.30 a.m. as you arrive at the suburban terraced house up
the road. The door is ajar and you can hear the babble of kids'
voices and a peal of laughter from the lounge. People say "Hi!" as
you pour a cup from the coffee jug and grab a piece of Doreen's
flap-jack. Five year old Maisie wants you to inspect her new doll
and satisfied with your exclamations of appreciation moves on.
You chat with Alan who has recently moved into the area and
talk sport. An arrangement to play snooker on Tuesday is made
as the hosts, Mick and Julie, come and sit down having satisfied
everyone's thirst for coffee.

Julie strums the guitar quietly and the kids are called through.
After a prayer by Mick one of the children asks for a song as the
meeting rolls seamlessly from fellowship into worship. There are
thirteen people there today: four children, two couples, two single
guys, and three single women. One of the men is an unchurched
neighbor who met this group when they had a skittles night a couple
of weeks back. Over the next 30 minutes all, but two of them have
contributed by way of a song, a reading, a prayer or a spiritual gift
(this week there is a prophecy and a tongue and interpretation).

Frank begins to teach about prayer by asking everyone to say
where they are at. There are varied (honest!) responses and Frank
gives some very practical suggestions from Jesus' teaching in
Luke 11. The kids are engaged as he has brought a plastic snake and
a (real!) kipper to illustrate the Bible passage. The session ends with
people praying in pairs for help in growing in their prayer life. You
pray with eleven-year-old Doug who, in turn, prays for you simply
but strongly and even gives you a verse!

As the meeting breaks up and the kids resume playing, a
couple of folks counsel and pray for one of the ladies who is going
through a tough time at work. Eight of the group stay on for a

soup and roll lunch. An enjoyable end to an encouraging and refreshing morning.

Variety Is the Spice of (Church) Life!

Our voyage of discovery has led us to value equally both local home based meetings and "altogether" times (in a hired community hall). Whilst we have tried different combinations including meeting fortnightly in our homes, I believe that the approach that will develop the strongest home churches is to meet three times a month in homes, then altogether for a monthly celebration. The home gatherings are then regular enough to meaningfully draw in local people. With the celebration being only monthly, giving it a sense of occasion, this can be more than a two hour meeting, but perhaps a half day together incorporating worship, teaching, kids and youth sessions, corporate prayer, lunch and games.

In a recent sabbatical I visited a number of churches over a twelve week period. I was taken aback by two things. One was the "sameness" of what went on in terms of style, length and even choice of songs. The other was the palpable sense of boredom and passivity among many in the congregations. They knew what would happen and that it was the same last week and that it would be next too. The shocking thing is that these were, for the most part, charismatic churches reputedly at the vanguard of radical renewal.

After three years of experimenting with a mixture of home church and monthly celebration meetings I could not go back. Church leaders shouldn't say things like this, but coming together week after week with the same predictable pattern of meeting is stultifyingly boring! Yet variety means we approach each gathering with unsated appetite valuing what the contrasting settings offer with fresh anticipation.

The joy of variety is precious. Developing home church meetings has done wonders in developing deep friendships, encouraging spiritual gifts and body ministry, making space for new leaders and breaking down generational and social barriers. The last of these is what we turn to consider now as we examine more "grassroots."

References

[1] 1 Corinthians 1:2 (New International Version).
[2] See *New Bible Dictionary*, page 200, paragraph 1.
[3] Michael Green, *Evangelism in the Early Church*, Hodder and Stoughton, 1970.
[4] Howard A. Snyder, *Radical Renewal—The Problem of Wineskins Today*, Touch Publications, 1996.
[5] See 1 Timothy 3:2; Titus 1:8.
[6] Brother Yun with Paul Hattaway, *The Heavenly Man*, Monarch Books, 2002.
[7] Ibid.
[8] 2 Chronicles 6:18.
[9] Ephesians 2:22.
[10] Acts 17:24.
[11] 1 Peter 2:5.

3

The Generation Game
The Grassroots Community

*Three small schoolboys were talking in the playground.
"My Dad's a teacher, he makes me clever for nothing," said
one. Not to be outdone his friend chimed "My Dad's an
athlete, he makes me fast for nothing." They looked at the
last boy who finally exclaimed triumphantly, "My Dad's a
vicar he makes me good for nothing!"*

Reading Between the Lines

The Bible is fascinating not only for what it says but also for what
it does not say! You can examine sixty-six books written over a four
thousand year period without coming across a single reference to a
Sunday school or youth group. In fact same-age groups of any kind
are conspicuous by their absence.

(The nearest thing to a youth group is found in 2 Kings 2:23,
when a group of Jericho youths follow Elisha, not to hear his
wisdom but to mock his baldness. Possibly lacking in grace, Elisha
calls a couple of bears to maul the mob—not youth worker material
perhaps!)

Yet one of the first questions that occurs for an emerging church is "what shall we do with the children?" The reality is that institutional church meetings are built around adult needs rather than being a family that caters for all ages and stages. The result, almost always, is "bolt on" children's groups that separate generations and violate against the development of true community. It creates practical problems too as often "put upon" children's workers become isolated from the church's other ministry, whilst those not involved with kids work are starved of interaction with the young.

The kingdom of God shatters barriers that exist between neighbors, nations, and generations. "Jesus," Paul declares, (when considering racial divides) *is our peace, who has made the two one and has destroyed the barrier.* [1] We erect new barriers at our peril and to our own loss.

How do we value children?

D.L. Moody, the outstanding American Evangelist of the nineteenth century once quizzically remarked: "Two and a half people were saved in my meeting today." His colleagues thought for a moment then spoke "Ah! You mean two adults and a child." Moody responded with a twinkle, "No two children with their whole lives before them, and an adult whose life is half spent!" Their assumption revealed an age-old error that Jesus would have no truck with—that lack of years corresponds to lack of value.

"Let the little children come to me, and do not hinder them, for the kingdom of heaven belongs to such as these" [2] instructed our king when faced with the petty prejudice of his self-important followers.

It is very human to admire strength, eloquence, influence and sophistication, the very qualities that children in their naturalness and naivety are oblivious to. But the kingdom of heaven works in reverse—and the church must too. In grassroots movements of God, the children are in the vanguard of what God's Spirit is doing.

An Inclusive Approach

The world—ruled as it is by the rejected being, Satan—loves to exclude, "You're too old. . .too young. . .not clever enough. . .too scruffy. . .too poor. . .the wrong sex. . .the wrong race. . ."

The church by contrast—ruled as it is by the ultimate acceptor, Father God—loves to include: "All ages. . .all abilities. . .all backgrounds. . .both sexes. . .all people groups." The challenge to us as the church is to *accept one another, then, just as Christ accepted you, in order to bring praise to God.*[3] This chapter will examine this acceptance with particular emphasis on children in the church as well as some application to social background and race.

Mixing up the ingredients

Do you enjoy eating raw egg, uncooked flour or a plateful of butter? No, me neither. But a freshly baked cake, that's another matter! In recent years church growth theory has often promoted the idea of "homogeneous groups." In plain English that means churches comprised of people of the same age or race or social status, hence the promotion of "Youth Churches," "Stockbrokers' Churches" and "Black Churches." Rather than be challenged and enriched by the joy of mingling with other generations, backgrounds and races to create a rich blend of ingredients, they become one dimensional, self-absorbed and culturally isolated from other believers.

How opposite is this approach to the true spirit of the church. As Paul instructs the Galatians, *There is neither Jew nor Greek, slave nor free, male nor female, for you are all one in Christ Jesus.*[4] He might have added "neither old nor young" but, given the fact that Middle Eastern culture never separated the generations anyway, Paul probably felt he didn't need to!

This chapter will contrast the traditional "Sunday school" approach with the intergenerational model that appears to be the biblical norm (as well as what tends to happen in most developing nations). Let's look at the five main purposes of the church in this light:

Evangelism: I'm often surprised at how many Christian parents are content to see their children "Christianized" (in terms of their outward behavior or religious observance) rather than saved (that is changed from within). The gospel is theirs too! A survey of adult Christians taken many times in a variety of settings reveals strikingly similar results. 90 percent of believers claim to have made their first Christian commitment between the ages of four and fourteen. Yet we are inclined to put 90 percent of our efforts into adult orientated evangelism. (Why I wonder? Maybe because we see adults as "assets" —they tithe and can serve—but children as "liabilities"!)

In the traditional approach to children's ministry the emphasis is on academic knowledge and having a fun program. Children learn many stories, songs and memory verses and generally enjoy the experience until aged 10–12. If by this time they have not had a meaningful encounter with God and understood and responded to the gospel, the lure of the world and compulsion of peer pressure is likely to prove irresistible.

With an intergenerational approach, especially in a smaller home based setting, children are exposed to spiritual realities and power in a way that structured kids' groups can rarely deliver. They see first hand the fruit of salvation and the devastation of turning from God and are urged along with the rest to "believe and be baptized." Rather than having a tokenized view of becoming a Christian, they understand instinctively that discipleship is implicit.

It has been my joy to baptize numerous children of 8–12 years old, and see many of them powerfully baptized in the Holy Spirit. I was privileged myself to be filled with the Spirit at nine and baptized at ten. Encouraged by my parents to take part in "adult" home meetings as a young child I saw lives changed, demons expelled, miraculous healings and the horrific consequences of backsliding. It was this knowledge and experience, more than anything I learned in Sunday school, which kept me walking with God through the turbulent, temptation-filled teen years.

Discipleship: Kids are sponges. (No I don't mean financially—well, perhaps I do, but that's another subject!) I mean they soak up what is happening around them and have an inbuilt instinct to imitate what others do. How vital it is therefore that we expose them to people with spiritual maturity and true passion for God. It is a tragedy when children are removed from meaningful contact with older members of the church family in the mistaken belief that a school approach to discipleship will bring lasting change. Instead of aspiring to imitate those they admire as role models, they are thrown together in peer groups which seems to bring the worst out of even the most angelic children!

God has created a way of shaping the lives of children that we might describe as "aspirational" learning. It begins as small children when little lads follow Dad around copying with their plastic tools what Dad is doing (or trying to) with the real thing. Girls want to be like Mum, boys want to copy Dad. (I felt a bit sorry for my six- year-old as I found him sifting through huge piles of paper on his desk. "What are you doing with all that son?" I enquired. "I'm being a church leader like you Dad" was his disarming response!)

As they grow, some of that aspiration—hero worship almost transfers to other role models. If all they have is relationships with their peer group then role models are likely to be the loudest, most forceful and often rebellious person around. If however, they have had the opportunity—through being part of an all age church community—of fostering "older sibling," "aunt/uncle" and "grandparent" type relationships, they will observe, absorb and adopt good character naturally, and often unconsciously.

So in Scripture we see, at the fringe of Jesus' disciples a young lad, called Mark. He follows Peter everywhere (I can imagine his Mum, Mary, worrying what scrapes the audacious fisherman would be getting her boy into next). So when Peter follows the arrested Jesus to the high priest's courtyard, the youngster is not far behind and escapes arrest only by leaving his clothes behind! But read Mark's Gospel. See what he saw in his formative years, either in person or through the first account reports of his big mate Pete.

And didn't kids love being around Jesus? I can imagine them watching, listening, wandering off for a run around with their pals, coming back, listening some more, having a kip, asking Mum and Dad what the parables meant, being astounded by the miracles and not wanting to go home at the end of the day! Have you ever wondered how many of the three thousand saved and baptized on the day of Pentecost were children and youths who had previously met Jesus?

Our experience has been that children's groups have had some value especially up to the age of about thirteen. Then most youngsters will drift away. It's not wasted of course, seeds have been sown which we pray will bear fruit in later life. But how much better to have built lasting relationships which hold young people in the heart of the church during their most vulnerable and formative years?

Ministry: "Breakages must be paid for" is a message that sends a chill through any parent taking their children shopping. Looking isn't enough for children—they want to DO! (So should all of us actually.) They quickly tire of having to watch and listen, but love to fulfill tasks and play their part. Whilst many adults have grown content to be passive in a meeting setting, children will become bored and will disengage if they cannot contribute in some way.

One of the most moving and satisfying aspects of our journey from structured front-led church to flexible body-life church, is the way children have naturally moved in the Spirit and used their gifts.

Teaching them not to just choose their favorite song, but to listen to the Spirit has been a revelation—they hear God! Being taught (with good insights) by a budding twelve-year-old preacher has been humbling as has hearing kids' testimonies of answered prayer. Just recently a girl of ten years shared about a distressing problem with a schoolmate. As the church gathered to pray for her she received gentle wisdom from several in the meeting, and then a knee buckling impartation of the Holy Spirit that filled her with joy, peace and praise. Within a week the problem at school was resolved, but her new fervency for the Lord has remained.

We can receive so much too. I lost my father to cancer in 2004, and a few months later I was still struggling, not only with the loss, but also the trauma of the final stages of his illness. In the home meeting one week, a seven-year-old girl who, if I'm honest didn't appear to be taking part much that day suddenly said, "Where's my Bible? There's something I want to read." After retrieving it from her bedroom, she read, unprompted by any adult, the words of Revelation 21:4, *"He will wipe every tear from their eyes. There will be no more death or mourning or crying or pain. . . ."* Somehow, far more than if the words had come from a wise, older believer, these truths entered my heart with power to heal and to comfort.

One of my concerns about the charismatic scene in the UK is the amount of churches that have opted to separate the children from the adults for the worship section of the meeting (apart from maybe the first 10–15 minutes). Instead of allowing the children to see and experience spiritual gifts at work, and begin to use them themselves, it's off for fun and games in the kids' club. Now I love fun and games, but they must not replace children's joy in worship or the thrill to play their part in the Spirit to build up the church.

Please don't misunderstand me. I so appreciate all those who serve children in running groups of all kinds. It's all very worthwhile. But let me challenge you to see, and prove for yourself, the benefits of an approach to children which integrates them with the whole church and allows them to give as well as receive.

Fellowship: "I can't stand children" is a shocking admission I have heard uttered by several adult believers over the years. What I think they mean is "I find it hard to relate to children or young people, so I'm going to stay away from them." It is certainly an issue for more than would admit it and helps to fuel the "demographic apartheid" that most churches practice.

In this generation more than any before, with the disintegration of the extended family, we need the church to be just that. Our experience has shown that we need to do two things if the church is to resemble the family community God intended it to be.

One is to teach people the need and ability to relate between generations. One friend in the church recently complained about the smallness of a meeting by stating that there were only five people present. On further enquiry it transpired that there were five adults present, but eight people in all. The three under tens, it appears, did not count. We have had to teach adults to not only notice children in the church, but also to greet them and take an interest in their lives. We have also had to inspire parents to train their children to greet adults and get beyond the "there's not many other children there for my kids to play with" gripe, and instead learn to foster rich relationships with the adults there!

We need to appreciate that in our modern age where people live such separate lives (we live in brick boxes, drive to work in tin cans and do office work in glass bowls), many have never learned how to relate beyond their immediate nuclear family (and often a relationally dysfunctional family at that). When people get saved as well as learning the truths of the faith, many need to be taught the rudiments of good relationship building. Teaching people to smile, say "hello," address others by their names, ask interested questions, to listen properly, to be encouraging, to offer practical help and to open their homes to others are a few of the things which up to fifty years ago were learned as common courtesy in the family and community.

The second necessity is to create a setting in which different age groups mingle. A wonderful exchange takes place when generations mix. Stuffy, work weary adults relax and become fun to be with, and self-absorbed, uncommunicative kids mature socially and learn to play their vital part in the church. One of my favorite times in a home meeting is the half hour "coffee and cake time" we start with; seeing Jake (aged nine) playing draughts with Alec (aged fifty-nine); watching my teenaged son in deep theological discussion with a single guy in his thirties who has a passionate love for God. Looking on as six-year-old Mandy who a year ago was "glued" to her Mum and wouldn't talk to anyone else—sitting on the lap of sixty-year-old Jean as naturally as if she were her own grandmother.

One of the joys of traveling to Africa, South East Asia and Eastern Europe is to see how well their more relational and family orientated societies cultivate intergenerational church life. One leaf we've borrowed from their book is to dispense with late evening "cell" groups and replacing them with early evening meetings.

Typically now we meet at 5.30 p.m. for a simple meal in the mid week. Those arriving later from work having a meal put by, with the main part of the meeting, whether prayer, teaching, worship or fellowship running from 6.30 p.m. for an hour or so. Families with small children might leave promptly, while those in no rush can stay on until past 8.00 p.m. and adult-orientated chat can take place.

The result is that instead of having one person from a family of four attending a cell meeting separate from their marriage partner and children, we can have all four. Relationships can blossom between all in the church, and spiritual growth becomes a family event rather than an individualistic process.

Worship: I have left until last what is, in fact, the first duty of believer and church—to worship God with everything we have got! *From the lips of children and infants you have ordained praise*[5] says the psalmist! Why is it that children have such a special place in worship? Here are some suggestions:

• Children have not lost their sense of wonder.
• They are naturally exuberant and unself-consciously expressive.
• Kids don't need to understand something to appreciate it.
• "The kingdom of heaven belongs to such as these."
• Young people have a disarming sincerity about them.
• Children are confident of receiving God's Spirit.
• They are generally very natural and unreligious.
• They aren't pre-occupied with saying "the right thing."
• Young people say things simply and get to the point.
• Children don't act, they worship Monday to Saturday too!

When Jesus addressed adults about relating to God, he said they must *"change and become like little children."*[6] The trouble with most churches is we get that the wrong way round! Trying to make children become like adults with all our dullness and reserve. Don't we have an amazing way of taking the most awesome life-enhancing experience— relating to Almighty God in love, joy and thankfulness and turning it into the most stilted, sanctimonious performance?

Genuinely incorporating kids into participating in worship is an antidote to the three great enemies of Spirit empowered worship—traditionalism, religiousness and sentimentality. Children are not obsessed with whether something "fits" into the meeting, but in expressing it. Here's a health warning though; if you truly want children (and adults) released into free worship, be prepared to jettison that much vaunted yet non–New Testament role of worship leader and truly let the Spirit lead your meetings (see chapter 7).

Jesus the Wall Demolisher

Having considered the generation gap, let's consider other divides which are bridged as grassroots Christianity flourishes. Have you noticed how Jesus loved breaking restrictive social conventions? Let's look at Luke (interestingly the only non Jewish New Testament author). We find Jesus:

- Worshiped by shepherds, of low social order, who were told about his coming ahead of leaders, royal and religious (2:8).
- Welcomed by a widow in her eighties (2:36).
- Choosing disciples who included a Roman collaborator and an anti-Roman terrorist, I wonder how they got on! (6:15).
- Healing the servant of a Roman occupier (7:9).
- Allowing a prostitute follow him into a Pharisee's home, valuing her worship more highly than his host's respect (7:36).
- Shocking hearers by talking of a "good" Samaritan! (10:25).
- Castigating the corrupt religious establishment (11:37).
- Breaking legalistic views of the Sabbath by healing (13:10).
- Causing great embarrassment at an "important" meal by showing up the guests' conceited upward mobility (14:1).
- Honoring a Samaritan who showed true gratitude (17:11).
- Saving and eating with a corrupt Roman collaborator (19:1).

Moving on, the story of Acts is one in which the Gospel repeatedly "jumps" over social and racial divides. As Jesus' followers we need to ensure that our church communities reflect the all inclusive love and acceptance that our Master exemplified in his ministry.

Is your church reputed to be "middle class," or perhaps a church for young families? Does your membership reflect the ethnic make-up of your locality, are singles made as welcome as families? If you do include different social groups, do they mix together well or is your church a collection of separate "cells" of like-minded people?

The power of the Gospel is most effectively demonstrated by

a bunch of socially disparate people whom God has forged into a devoted community regardless of intellect, wealth or background. Individuals are then cherished for the persons God made them to be and the deep bond is found in love for God, not superficial social conventions.

I love looking round our group. Retired police officer, next to an ex drug-user, chatting to a farmer's daughter, sitting next to a retired London lawyer, who is listening to a schoolboy's joke; then an Indian born woman praying for an elderly single lady, and a young Mum chatting with a jobbing gardener and an immigration officer. What beautiful variety, and they all love God and all love each other!

Good News for the Poor?

The trend of Christian movements through the ages is to begin among working people only to quickly evolve into middle class enclaves in which disadvantaged people are less comfortable.

I recently spoke about ministry to the poor at a lovely church in Southern England. After the meeting I was approached by a tearful, distraught lady called Mary ("Hey," I thought, "the sermon wasn't that bad was it?"). It transpired, just as I was encouraging the church to be more inclusive of those who might be described as the "humble" or "despised" poor, that Mary, from a disadvantaged background herself had been considering leaving the church because, she explained, "My life is so different from everyone else. I just don't fit in." The following lines convey how she was feeling:

> Some days I feel I don't belong. . .
> I've no silver car with a Christian fish,
> Or a smart town house with satellite dish;
> Or the means to pay for the simplest wish,
> Some days I feel I don't belong.

Sometimes I feel they're better than me. . .
They're all happy couples sitting hand in hand,
With nicely dressed children who don't demand;
They have decent jobs, they'd never understand.
Some times I feel they're better than me.

Some nights I feel I can't go on. . .
I'm alone trying to raise the kids I've had,
The way it turned out they've all a different Dad,
Who hardly ever visit—makes us all so sad.
Some nights I feel I can't go on.

Some Sundays I feel so left out. . .
Over coffee I walk past their conversations,
Making plans for visits to exclusive locations,
Standing by as they make their dinner invitations.
Some Sundays I feel so left out.

Some weeks I feel I've got no gifts. . .
I lack the confidence to say what's on my mind,
Having dropped out of school I feel so left behind;
I want to play my part, if there's a role I can find.
Some weeks I feel I've got no gifts.

Thank God some days I know I fit in. . .
As I read in the Gospels about my Savior,
How he accepted everyone without fear or favor,
So willing to forgive each one their past behavior
Thank God I now know I fit in.

It was a privilege to be able to give the lie to her condemning feelings, but the fact is that her church has to make serious adjustments before Mary will feel she truly belongs.

A great strength of the grassroots church is that many of the impulses that lead to a middle class ethos, (emphases on plush buildings, intellectual communication, polished music and smart presentation) are negated. The culture of the informal church is expressedly accepting of all, and each person contributes their "flavor" to the group as a whole.

Building a Mosaic Church

When I visited an Albanian Church in Tirana in 2003, we sat in a circle in a courtyard with a lovely group of believers. As I looked down during the worship I had a vivid picture of a mosaic on the ground. It was an intricate picture crafted out of hundreds of small pieces, all of them different, some you might even call misshapen, of a vast spectrum of colors. Yet the beauty of the picture was dependent on the variety of the pieces. I felt God say that this would be a church that would become beautiful through its ability to welcome all kinds of people, young and old, rich and poor, educated and self-taught, from all ethnic groups. Unlike most churches in the capital, this group began an outreach among the despised Roma population. When I visited the church three years on, the beauty and love are breathtaking as is the breadth of variety of people and their enthusiasm in taking part.

What a Shower!

In 1 Corinthians 1, Paul writes to a cosmopolitan sea-port church and tells them how God loves to use the "the weak. . .the foolish . . .the lowly."[7] The grassroots churches that God is raising up will not be built on great management, highly trained leadership, expensive facilities and eloquent communicators. Instead, they will be built on the power of God poured through ordinary, weak, broken people, who respect, love and serve one another and make room for one another's gifts to be used.

For this to happen, there needs to be a profound review of how leadership works. A fresh look at the New Testament and a questioning of our institutional church heritage will reveal some startling insights into the purpose and style of biblical leadership. Which is what we turn our attention to now.

References
[1]Ephesians 2:14.
[2]Matthew 19:14.
[3]Romans 15:7.
[4]Galatians 3:28.
[5]Psalm 8:2.
[6]Matthew 18:3.
[7]1 Corinthians 1:27–28.

4

Leading Questions
The Grassroots Leader

Two pastors were discussing body ministry when one asked, "What parts of the body do your congregation remind you of?" With a sigh his friend replied, "They all resemble the appendix." His colleague could not hide his surprise, "Why's that?" he quizzed. "Because they have no obvious purpose and grumble a lot!"

What would you like on your gravestone?

Over the years I have occasionally taken part in an ice-breaker called "Gravestones" where you say how you would like to be remembered. It is a stimulating (if somewhat morbid) activity and helpful in enabling one to take stock. As a leader I have produced much eloquent nonsense along the lines of my achievement; "He was a breath-taking preacher. . .his words were like water to a drowning man" and such-like. Then a few years ago the penny dropped as I realized the true heart of Christian leadership. What would I want on the mossy headstone now? My choice would be "Here lays an encourager who sought to bring out the best in everyone." Oh, that I might live up to that aspiration!

Follow That!

I have many Christian heroes. There is C.T. Studd, the England cricketer turned missionary who gave up his fortune to pioneer the gospel in India, China and Africa. Then C.H. Spurgeon, the "Prince of Preachers" who stood powerfully against the liberal onslaught of the late nineteenth century that followed Darwin's theories. Also, John Wesley, who threw off the shackles of institutional Anglicanism to see the nation reached through a gospel centered, discipleship based movement of grassroots communities. (Incidentally, it was Wesley's successors, not the man himself, who calcified this organic move of God by forming it into a building centered denomination.) I could go on to mention more, but as the writer to the Hebrews observed "I do not have time to tell about. . ." William Carey, James Hudson Taylor, Dwight L. Moody, and many others.

So what do these men have in common that they inspire such esteem? They were all multipliers. They were not motivated by status or personal achievement. In fact, to a man, they were vilified by the religious establishment of their day and considered pariahs by most. But as well as blazing trails, they all drew others along in their wake; training, enabling and handing over responsibilities.

What a bunch of heretics!

We are rightly very intolerant of error as it pertains to most areas of Christian doctrine, for example our understanding of God, sin, salvation, Scripture and eternal destiny. Yet we have put up with an understanding of leadership that has been marred by genuine heresy, and therefore caused far more harm than good. Instead of imparting maturity, responsibility, unity and effectiveness, the institutional leader—whether through personal choice or the expectations of others—too often creates passivity and frustration.

This chapter will contrast the biblical concept of leadership with several faulty models we encounter both in historical denominations as well as the modern charismatic evangelical scene. It will go on to suggest practical characteristics of a new breed of leader who will become more prevalent as the burgeoning grassroots movement multiplies across the globe in these last days.

Please note that there is no criticism of individuals inherent in this section. It has been my privilege to meet so many godly, sincere and gifted leaders. Yet it has been tragic to see so many of them imprisoned by "the system" which has put unbiblical expectations and restraints upon them. It is time to risk offense and challenge the human control that has weakened the church for centuries through inculcating defective, worldly leadership patterns.

The Genuine Article

It is said of bank cashiers, that in order to recognize fake notes, they spend time familiarizing themselves, not with forgeries, but with the real thing. We have all been brought up with leadership models that are far from the biblical pattern and have tacitly accepted them as normative. We need now to look at the genuine article in Scripture in order to discern how far our leadership "genes" have "mutated," and so be motivated to seek a fresh injection of biblical DNA into our current practice.

In His Steps

The church is the body of Christ, and it is to him, rather than the Old Testament authority figures of Moses, Samuel, David or Daniel that we should concentrate our gaze as we seek for a model. Here are some characteristics of Jesus' leadership we need to emulate:

a) **Relational:** Jesus chose twelve disciples to do what? *That they might be with him. . . .*[1] For three years they were together; eating, talking, walking, working, resting, praying and playing. Only in simple grassroots church forms do leaders have time to do what Jesus showed was of the essence—spending time with their people.

b) Empowering: The verse above continues, "and that he might send them out to preach." For years I have tried to encourage and train many in our church to teach and preach as well as to pastor, serve, evangelize and prophesy. If I had a pound for every time a well-meaning member has asked me to preach more because I was "the one most gifted," I would be able to afford my own TV ministry by now. As pleasing (though sadly inaccurate!) as the compliment may be, I can only preach now because someone took a risk with me and gave me numerous opportunities to make a dog's dinner of it while coaching me on how to improve.

Note how early in Jesus' training he sent the disciples out to preach (Mark 6). And Luke shows us that it is but a short time later that seventy-two are sent out. These are unschooled fishermen and farmers for the most part. They of all people could have said, "No Jesus, you're the person who can really teach, you're the one people want to hear." Yet they obeyed with powerful results, *The seventy-two returned with joy and said, "Lord, even the demons submit to us in your name."* [2] Jesus entrusted the message of the kingdom to rustic, untrained people, and was quick to send them out. They could not be confident in their training or skill—they had so little, but they depended on the Spirit's empowering and authority of Jesus' words.

c) An example: At the heart of Jesus' ministry was the command "follow me." So whether we need to learn to work hard with our hands, endure suffering with perseverance, trust God for His provision or forgive our enemies, we can look—not just to Jesus' words but also to his life. Many leadership models, especially professional "ministry," removes people so far from the lifestyles of those they serve that their example is either irrelevant or invisible.

d) A servant: *"The Son of Man did not come to be served, but to serve"* [3] Jesus tells us. He applied this uncompromisingly to leadership when he taught *"If anyone wants to be first, he must be the very last, and the servant of all."* [4] Now to get this outrageous statement in perspective we need to expunge from our minds images of "Jeeves and Wooster" or "Upstairs, Downstairs" and the middle class concept of "service." In Jesus' time, a servant was pretty well owned by his master, he was "low-profile" to the point of invisibility, and he existed to notice and fulfill the requirements of those he served. As leaders we must abandon status, shun selfish ambition, relinquish comfort and resist being controlling. Instead we rejoice in others' elevation, delight in unrecognized service, revel in making sacrifices and excel in releasing others into fruitful ministry. On the eve of his arrest, Jesus knew how the human inclination to seek self-promotion would threaten the fledgling church; so he washed his disciples' feet. . . *"I have set you an example that you should do as I have done for you."* [5] Let it be so.

Naturally Not Super, But Super-Naturally!

I love the atmosphere of the church as described in the New Testament! Whether in Acts or the Epistles, the vibrancy, earthiness, flexibility and, yes, vulnerability of this amazing earth-bound-yet-heaven-headed body shines through.

The overriding impression we receive is of the life of God resonating within a group of very ordinary, unreligious people with all their tendency to error and immaturity. Rather than "clamp down" on these upstarts and institute trained leadership who can do the stuff properly, Paul affirms the life and brings gentle direction.

C.J. Mahaney[6] has observed that, if he'd written to the Corinthians, his epistle would be very short. Verse 1 "C.J. to the church in Corinth"; verse 2 "Stop it!"; verse 3 "Now!" What does Paul write? *I always thank God. . .for in him you have been enriched . . .in all your speaking and knowledge. . . . Therefore you do not lack any spiritual gift.* [7] He goes on to describe a form of church worship where *To each one the manifestation of the Spirit is given for the common good* [8] and where in meetings *everyone has a hymn, or a word of instruction, a revelation, a tongue or an interpretation.* [9]

The kind of leadership Paul affirms is from people of good character who are positive examples and who can oversee the wonderful life of God as it is expressed by everyone in the church.

The qualifications for eldership as described in 1 Timothy 3 and Titus 1 are illuminating in this regard. Paul wasn't after the "highly gifted" or "inspirational leader" type. He was after sound blokes who lived decently and cared for their families well. How many good people spend their church lives as "pew fodder" because we have created an unbiblical leader/people divide, where there is an almost unsurpassable gulf between the highly trained, intelligent and eloquent leader on one side and the poor "plebs" on the other?

The reason Paul sought out "good ordinary people" to lead is, I'm convinced, because leadership is about enabling everyone to minister, rather than being "The Minister." (That incidentally is at best a nonsensical title and at worst a heretical one, given the scriptural imperative that we are all ministers.) The thrust of New Testament teaching about ministry can be best described as "one anothering," rather than "sitting under" one person's ministry (what a dreadful phrase!).

This distinction between leadership and ministry also helps take the heat out of the controversy over male and female roles. If all the members are freed to play their part to the full it matters less if it is only the men who are eligible to be saddled with the humble and often onerous task of servant leadership!

There was no king in Israel

Some might ask, "Do we need leaders at all then?" Absolutely! Though, not to dominate, but to give a framework of unity so that everyone's unique and vital contribution can be encouraged and harnessed for great corporate fruitfulness.

Adherents of egalitarianism (which applies the truth that we are all equal before God in a way that questions any kind of leadership), struggle to come to terms with the order that God has clearly put into relationships in the family, the state and the church. But when a true appreciation of sacrificial, servant leadership is experienced many such misgivings are quickly dispelled.

Two Helpful Parallels

I used to work on a factory assembly line. There were seven in our section and we had a supervisor. He was "one of us" as part of the workforce, but had the added responsibility of drawing our diverse contributions together to achieve a common aim—the finished product. He, a) communicated the management's instructions to us, b) set an example by working hard himself, c) made sure we had the tools, parts and training we needed and d) helped resolve the occasional dispute that arose and built team unity. This is such a good picture of effective church leadership:

• A good leader is "one of the people."
• He is accountable to God seeking to follow the Spirit's leading.
• He sets the tone by his own example.
• He enables every member to excel in his or her gifting.
• He promotes unity by team building and conflict resolution.

A similarly helpful picture I heard used by my friend Andy Leakey who is pioneering a grassroots church in Bath, England. He describes leadership as being a "Player Coach" in the footballing sense. He's in the action, setting the tone, giving shape to the team, but happy to sit on the bench for some of the match to give room to new players, and "oversee" the team's performance giving encouragement and advice where needed.

What about the "A" word?

Authority: It's a word that strikes fear into many, confusion in others, and obsession in a few. Church history seems to have oscillated between rampant individualism on one hand and crushing authoritarianism on the other. How do we find the healthy biblical balance that God intends?

Jesus explicitly instructed his disciples that they should not exercise authority over those they led. He described the Gentile rulers' authoritative leadership style and unequivocally stated *"Not so with you"*[10] and went on to describe godly leadership as servant-hood. This teaching should inform the ethos of all of our leadership; it is gentle, low profile, sacrificial and elevating of others.

But surely leaders of this kind open the church to all kinds of impostors usurping the lead and bringing in heresy and godlessness? Actually, the only times we see Paul "flexing his muscles" is when addressing issues of error and immorality. Paul hardly uses the word "authority" about himself, but when He does—almost exclusively in 2 Corinthians 10:8; 13:10, it is in the context of protecting the church against these twin threats.

Even then, interestingly, in both the above references, Paul defines his authority as God given "for building you up and not tearing you down." The most common biblical picture for a leader, that of shepherd, is so helpful here. He is gently directive, and sacrificially protective towards the sheep, leading them into good pasture so they can grow and reach their potential. Yet he is absolutely ruthless with the wolf or the bear.

How often has damage been caused when a leader has sought to "lord it over" their people? Using harsh correction, manipulating people through guilt and legalism, and seeking to protect his own position and frustrating opportunities of gifted people through fear.

A true and wholesome use of authority is not telling people what they should or should not do (except where absolutely necessary to protect the church or the vulnerable), in contrast it is to promote maturity so people could have good values, make good decisions and in turn can instruct others.

It's time then to measure the "miter-stick" of institutional authority patterns against the yardstick of Scripture.

Do not call anyone on earth "Father"

The most obvious error when we consider leadership is that of appointing priests to represent "the people" before God. Scripture could not be clearer that Jesus is the only mediator between God and man. Catholic, Orthodox and Anglican (Episcopalian) appointments of priests, even with vast differences in practice between these traditions, represent a scandalous usurping of Jesus' unique, blood-bought role as the one through whom we have peace and relationship with God. The practices of confession and absolution epitomize the error that cuts across, literally, the crux of our faith, that God sent his Son to die on the cross so that through faith in him alone we can be forgiven and become sons of God.

The so-called clergy / laity divide has no foundation in Scripture and violates against the biblical concept of body ministry where Christ is the Head and there is genuine equality of every believer. To reserve certain tasks of ministry, such as celebrating breaking of bread and baptizing, to those of a certain "class" of Christian is an offense of exclusivity unbefitting the kingdom of God.

The challenge for believers in traditions governed by priestly office is, can they effectively challenge unscriptural patterns ingrained by many centuries of practice. Can biblical leadership norms emerge in such unpromising environments? Add to that a system where liberal, even unbelieving, clergy are appointed to lead congregations—begs the question, how can one submit to such leadership in good conscience before God?

Yes Minister?

It is said that football is a game where twenty-two thousand people in desperate need of exercise sit watching twenty-two people desperately in need of a rest! How like the next leadership model we consider.

For those of us more familiar with a non-conformist background (Baptist, Methodist, Congregational, Pentecostal and so on), we call the leader our "Minister." Studying in the mornings, visiting in the afternoons, preaching each Sunday, the fount of counsel to those in need, he is the one who "ministers." Whatever his gift, he will be expected to be an accomplished "one-man-band." As people passively "sit under" his ministry, their gifts barely recognized, still more rarely actually used, he rushes from one duty to another.

Howard Snyder makes the point with wit and wisdom in his chapter "Must Pastors Be Superstars?" in his classic, *The Problem of Wineskins.* His conclusion is, "looking at the lives of the members of Pastor Jones' church we make a startling discovery: Every one of Pastor Jones' talents is equaled or surpassed by someone in the membership. If a church must depend on pastoral superstars for growth, there is something drastically wrong with its structure, and more importantly, with its understanding of the church."[11]

Some ministers, buoyed by a true sense of vocation and being needed, thrive. Yet most quickly become burnt out by either overwork or the criticism that is directed at that most easy of targets. Those that survive longest are those who manage to introduce team ministry, a step towards—though falling far short of—the biblical pattern of every member ministry.

Yet at best, such a system achieves the 80/20 ratio (where 20 percent of the church can function in the gift God has given them, whilst 80 percent remain "Eddies"). Eddie incidentally was the slow moving shop assistant whose absence was noticed by a customer. "Who's going to fill Eddie's vacancy?" he asked the owner. "No one" was the reply, "When Eddie left he didn't leave a vacancy!"

Instead the Bible teaches us that every one is a minister. We see this in the three classic texts about gifts: In Romans 12 it is "each member" who "has different gifts"; in 1 Corinthians 12:7, it is "to each one that the manifestation of the Spirit is given"; and in Ephesians 4 :7 it is "to each one of us that grace has been given." Elsewhere[12] it is "one another," not an elite group, doing the work of ministry, even such demanding tasks as to "teach and admonish." We can confidently assert therefore that the main role of leaders is to oversee and release the ministry of all.

Give Us a King!

Turning our attention to newer church streams the desire so often is for "an anointed leader." This powerful character will combine strength of personality with impressive giftedness and so be able to inspire loyalty to his "vision." Sound familiar? Sound okay? It's funny though that the New Testament never describes any individual human as "anointed." In fact Christ or Messiah literally mean "The Anointed One" (that means recognized as Priest and King). Could it be that once again (as with human priests) we are elevating human leadership into realms reserved for the Lord Jesus?

It's so human to want an impressive leader. Israel was tired of Samuel's humility and faithful wisdom and demanded a king. Likewise Jesus' followers, even after three years with him, expected the servant king to suddenly transform into a warrior king. Somehow to have an outstanding, eloquent, forceful or socially venerated church leader can give those who follow him, a sense of esteem by association. Yet the Scriptures show time and again how God raises up the lowly—shepherds, fishermen, farmers as leaders. The unnerving truth is, that the more highly we esteem human leaders, the less we will be inclined to venerate and honor the Lord himself, and put our full trust and confidence in him.

Apostolics Anonymous!

In recent decades many churches have been blessed with the recognition that the gifts mentioned in Ephesians 4 (apostles, prophets, evangelists, pastors and teachers) are valid and effective today. Yet along with the blessing that good practice brings, much damage has been done by the abuses of some who bear such titles.

Rather than running shy of such potentially beneficial gifts, I suggest we discern the essential qualities of those gifts that enable them to operate in a healthy way. Here are some principles I offer for consideration, to help us explore these ministries with confidence.

These gifts are for the whole body, not an elite squad. The whole context of teaching on "Ephesians 4 ministries" is shaped by the opening verse of the passage, *But to each one of us grace has been given.*[13] This is not a special category of gift for an eminent group, but an expression of the Holy Spirit's gifts to every member.[14] I am yet to meet a believer who does not exhibit some measure of at least one of these gifts. The suggestion that, before fulfilling such roles as apostle or teacher one must be recognized or approved by a formal authority structure, introduces an element of human control alien to Scripture. The fact is that "gifts make room for themselves." In other words, we open our lives or church to the degree we recognize peoples' gift and esteem their character.

These are not permanent "offices" but a description of function. Gifts are apt to malfunction when we attach to them permanence and use them as titles. These terms in Scripture are not used to define peoples' position, but rather to describe peoples' performance. We should use them as descriptive nouns with freedom; "Sally's a gifted evangelist, she's always sharing her faith," but be averse to using them as a title. "Sally's our evangelist" implies that no one else can be, and can soon become a misnomer if Sally goes through a season when she becomes less active in reaching out.

These gifts imply ability to serve not a position of authority.

This is perhaps the nub of the issue, as ministry imposed rather than offered is always going to misfire. Additionally, the challenge for new church groupings in particular is that, as they grow, they will be tempted to use titles (especially "Apostle") as a means of establishing a hierarchical authority structure. Once that happens the knock-on effect is to become a protective elite, loath to recognize others with similar gifts for fear of relinquishing authority.

By contrast, in less formal church practice, we will welcome every gift because we are focusing on how the person is able to bless the church by promoting sound doctrine, encouragement, maturity, unity and skill. We defer to the gift not the position (in the same way as I defer to my plumber when I have a leaky radiator even though it's my house. He knows what he's doing!).

Singularly Plural

One final note before we consider practicalities. Leadership in Scripture is always plural. Paul instructed Titus to appoint "elders in every town.[15] Paul and Barnabas appointed elders in each of the churches in Antioch, Lystra and Iconium[16]; James instructed unwell people to call the elders of the church to pray for them[17]; and Paul tells Timothy to arrange recompense for *the elders* (plural) *who direct the affairs of the church* (singular).[18]

Yet almost without exception, there is one leader recognized in each church. If not called priest or minister he is often called "The Pastor" (as if no one else in the church could be recognized as having such a gift), and carries alone the care of the whole congregation. If there is (as in some larger churches) a pastoral team, there is almost unfailingly a "senior pastor" who again is singled out as being ultimately responsible.

Even in my own family of churches, where plurality of eldership is a valued principle, we have, perhaps unhelpfully coined the supra-biblical term "Lead Elder" for the one who is seen as more prominent, or gifted or responsible than the "following elders"! Despite being alien to the pages of Scripture, this distinction is (I've been told), the only really practical approach to church leadership.

My contention is that what is practical must always defer to what is biblical, and that our best attempt at following Scripture is to seek to appoint a number of men, who love God, care for their families well and who love the church, to "direct the affairs of the church" together as a team, with equality, mutual respect and deference.

Grassroots Leadership

If not the "priest," the "minister" or the "anointed leader," what will a new breed of grassroots leaders look like? Here are some pointers:

He will do ordinary work. The idea that to lead you need to be a full-time professional is as unbiblical as it is unhelpful. Even Paul, whose transient ministry and immense call could justify full funding, knew it was right to work hard as a tentmaker, and often refused to be subsidized from church funds. Jesus in his adult life, spent six years as a carpenter-builder for each one he spent preaching.

So much is made of "the laborer is worthy of his hire"[19] Scripture. We must remember that when Paul said this it was in the context of people being hired by the day, not our present-day "career" or "job-for-life" culture. The principle is good for rewarding people who put in lots of time to care for the church, with occasional gifts perhaps, or temporary or part-time recompense for particular tasks. It does not however imply indefinite full employment!

The rural Chinese church has expanded rapidly with leaders who, for the most part, are farmers. They farm at busy times of sowing and harvest, and serve the church in the quieter times. In Africa, there just isn't the money to support a full timer through tithes, and pastors often work in the fields or markets as well as the church. Amazing isn't it how God is moving so powerfully in these nations when they don't have the full timers we consider so necessary?

The disadvantages of employing full-time leaders are many:
- They become removed from the "real world" of work.
- The Body becomes passive ("we pay the pastor to do that").
- Money for the poor and world mission is "eaten up" when each full timer costs twenty or thirty thousand pounds a year.
- Church planting is slowed to snail pace simply through cost.
- Church leaders suffer more stress when they don't have the contrast of other (preferably more physical) work.
- Church activities and programs become unnecessarily complex as the leader has time to fill / a salary to justify.
- The example to "work hard with our hands"[20] is missing.

Tomorrow's leader will more likely have a small business that allows him the flexibility to undertake church activities and travel. He might be a driving instructor or music teacher or plumber who keeps a day free to fulfill the added tasks which leadership brings. Perhaps he has taken early retirement, or may do an education related job with extended holidays when events and activities can take place.

He will have a good reputation locally. Grassroots churches with their simplicity will allow leaders to be known in their street, village or town. Whether by playing cricket, a member of the darts team or local brass band, being a school governor or a member of neighborhood watch, or simply through friendliness and neighborliness, he will "have a good reputation with outsiders."[21]

Evangelism will be uncontrived as there will be a wealth of natural contacts to invite to socials, outreach events and church gatherings. The foundation of friendship and appreciation through knowing the real person—as opposed to observing the façade of "being a minister" will encourage a positive response.

He will be ordinary in terms of education and status. What astonished the onlookers after Pentecost was that "they were unschooled, ordinary men"[22] who spoke with such conviction and authority. What a contrast with today's typical church leader with his theology degree, cultured eloquence and academic aura. Many people I've approached to encourage them in preaching or taking other ministry opportunities have expressed fear of not being clever enough or sufficiently educated. What a shame many have been made to feel this way, when we look at those Jesus chose as his helpers!

The best eldership team I've worked with contained a self-employed fencer and a life-long welder with few qualifications (we had a dentist too, but even he was from a very ordinary background). They were great because people a) weren't in awe of their "great learning," b) knew they understood the real world of making ends meet, hassle on the shop floor and raising young families and c) illustrated that "ordinary" people often make extraordinary leaders!

He will have a sound family life. Most of Paul's considerations when choosing elders apply to personal character or family life and, oh yes, it's helpful if they can teach a bit too. For the institutional church with its complexity and sophistication, emphasis on qualities such as administrative prowess, management skill and communication abilities eclipse such domestic concerns. The upshot is either an epidemic of broken marriages and reputations, or a growing trend of toleration of personal failure similar to politicians who claim "private lives" have "nothing to do" with public office.

Compare that with the simple wisdom of Scripture that those who look after their own families well are likely to care for God's family too. There are two key points here—

i. How do we know who is a good husband and father? Only

in a style of church where people get to know one another well and are seen regularly in their home environment will reality be evident. After all which of us does not at times try to "keep up appearances" in public? This is such a strength of grassroots churches with their rejection of "professional" ministry and "sanctuary" mentalities.

ii. Only simple church forms prevent emotional burnout and overwork causing damage to leaders' home lives. Why do we choose as elders those whose marriages and parenting we admire and turn them into bad husbands and fathers through the demand we put on them? For years I expected myself and the team I was part of to work four or five evenings each week plus most of Sundays. We all had young families and demanding jobs. Evenings were packed with cell groups, leaders' meetings, youth nights, prayer, Alpha. All "important." All hard to miss.

It dawned on me just in time that my kids were growing up without me. The switch to simple church forms, where all the same "stuff"—prayer, worship, discipleship, outreach and so on could happen without an endless treadmill of evening meetings was a Godsend.

It's fantastic now to be at home most evenings, talking over meals, having unrushed family devotional times and getting time to help with the children's homework and fix the hoover. It means we have time and energy to be hospitable and, once or twice a week, share a church activity, a fellowship meal or early evening prayer together as a family.

How did church members respond to this? That God comes first, my family second and ministry responsibilities next? Hopefully it encourages them in their own commitment to their families, whether children or aging parents, to see that we don't need to "juggle" church and home but that caring for your family (whilst not idolizing them) is at the heart of being in God's kingdom.

It will also help avoid the unhelpful dependence on needing the "pastor on tap," and a realization that in a healthy church it is the mutual love between members of the Body that provides the greatest care. (Back in the days when I led as an "all singing all dancing pastor," several members told me they dreaded Mondays as I took that day off and was unavailable to them! I cringe to recall how I allowed such unhealthy dependence to emerge.)

Mission Possible

But can so-called "ordinary," untrained people, with jobs and family responsibilities really lead the church? Yes, but only if we rediscover the raw simplicity and natural lifestyle at the heart of early church life, which is what we turn our focus towards next.

References

[1]Mark 3:14.

[2]Luke 10:17.

[3]Matthew 20:28.

[4]Mark 9:35.

[5]John 13:15.

[6]From a sermon at Leaders' Conference, Brighton circa 1999.

[7]1 Corinthians 1:4–7.

[8]1 Corinthians 12:7.

[9]1 Corinthians 14:26.

[10]Mark 10:42–45.

[11]*Radical Renewal—The Problem of Wineskins Today,* Touch Publications 1996.

[12]Colossians 3:16.

[13]Ephesians 4:7.

[14]In describing these as the "Gifts of the Ascended Christ" some have suggested these ministries constitute a specific impartation for the few. I would assert, on the basis of John 16:7, that the gifts of the

Holy Spirit and those of the ascended Christ are one and the same, and that Romans 12, 1 Corinthians 12 & 14 and Ephesians 4 are parallel passages, with differences of emphasis but not of type. All three passages emphasize that the gifts are available to all believers.

[15]Titus 1:5.

[16]Acts 14:23.

[17]James 5:14.

[18]1 Timothy 5:17.

[19]1 Timothy 5:18 (King James Version).

[20]1 Corinthians 4:12.

[21]1 Timothy 3:7.

[22]Acts 4:13.

5

A Natural Lifestyle
The Grassroots Way of Life

The Preacher found a note from his wife in the pulpit. It said simply "K.I.S.S." Emboldened by this affectionate missive, he preached long and eloquently. When he got home and thanked his wife, she explained with a sigh , "Actually the note meant 'Keep It Simple Stupid!.' "

Stop the world I want to get off!

I'm a twenty-first century Christian, with a quick zip NIV,
A computerized concordance with a CD commentary;
They come in rather handy, when I've got the time to spare;
To fit in a five minute quiet time, between breakfast and drying my hair.

I'm a twenty-first century Christian with a good, fast-paced career;
Leave the house at seven each morning, it's dusk when I reappear.
I get a buzz from the adrenaline (and I guess the caffeine too).
And I've only had two ulcers (not bad aged forty-two).

I'm a twenty-first century Christian in my smart suburban home,
Spacious garden, plus a pond of course (complete with fishing gnome).
Saturday's the only time to mow the lawn and weed,
Wash the car and do the DIY—but I'd rather sit and read.

I'm a twenty-first century Christian, family values are my thing,
Though I haven't seen my wife to speak to, since that marriage seminar
                                                                last spring.
And the kids are growing quickly, their childhood is so fleeting,
Used to read to them at bedtime, now I rush out to the evening meeting.

I'm a twenty-first century Christian, I serve the church with all my
might, My free time a holy whirlwind of meetings every night.
Evangelism through friendship is the latest of recent trends,
I really got quite excited, then remembered I'd not any friends.

I'm a twenty-first century Christian, but what's it all about?
Life is one long treadmill, it makes me want to scream and shout!
There must be something in what Jesus said (after all he's always right),
When he said his yoke is easy and his burden it is light.

Take the Strain

We live in a world that is sick with stress. There are other names
for it of course; chronic fatigue, emotional burnout and anxiety
disorder, for example. Additionally, there is a vast number of
physical conditions caused or complicated by stress including high
blood pressure, insomnia, depression, digestive ulcers, heart disease
and impaired immunity.

Christians, ironically considering the "peace" which our faith
should bring, are more vulnerable to stress than most. Not only
do we have the normal responsibilities of work, home and family;
we also have a faith requiring sacrificial interaction with a hurting

world, an ethical framework that deters us from taking shortcuts "for an easy life," and a disciple-lifestyle that invites self-denial and hard work.

And then there's church. First there are the meetings; Sunday, cell group and the prayer meeting (how bad you're made to feel if you miss that). With the rotas (kids' club, greeting, coffee making and chair setting out), the pace starts to quicken. Follow that with almost weekly appeals in the notices for volunteers (soup kitchen, door-to-door, Alpha catering and holiday club) and the head is whirling. Add a stirring weekly sermon motivating you to spend more time with the Lord, with your family, with your Christian friends and, don't forget, your unsaved friends too; then the guilt trip is complete.

The response of an increasing number of Christians is to opt out of church life. Having burned out through extended excessive commitment to programs and duties that institutional church life demands, they have had enough. These folk aren't backsliding, rather side-stepping church life. Their faith remains intact, (though it will become increasingly weakened through isolation from other believers). It's just that church seems more hassle than its worth.

Others, by contrast, have adopted a quasi church lifestyle, meeting with their choice of Christian friends informally for mutual support, the deciding factor of the amount and type of gatherings being what the group finds helpful rather than any sense of mission or sacrifice.

Still others are continuing faithfully, with ever increasing risk of overheating, with high pace, energetic and demanding church programs. Recent developments like cell groups and Alpha, as well as being a source of blessing, add to the work burden to a point where long-term sustainability is highly questionable.

What's your ambition?

The striking thing about the church we read of in the New Testament is its simplicity and relation to everyday life. Rather than juggling "work and church" or "church and family" as if they were competing demands on our time and energy, being part of the church in a simple, mainly home based and informal way brought the kingdom of God into the realms of family, commerce and society.

Our modern church culture with its emphases on smart management, alluring public relation, motivating vision statements and goal orientation seems strangely out of step with Paul's words to the Thessalonian Church:

> Make it your ambition to lead a quiet life, to mind your own
> business and to work with your hands. . ., so that your daily
> life may win the respect of outsiders and so that you will not
> be dependent on anybody.[1]

The scenario Paul paints is of the scattered impact of salty, light-filled believers in their streets, workplaces and markets powerfully impacting outsiders. Far from exhorting this new church to "take Thessalonica for Jesus" with busying themselves with a door knocking campaign followed by a crowd pulling guest event at the local amphitheater, Paul says simply "live quiet lives." Be like Jesus in your daily life and people will notice and you'll have the time, and relationship, to lead them closer to God.

Remember You're a Member

Over the years what it means to be a church member has changed somewhat. In my early years (in the 1960s) the three expectations were to agree to a (very detailed) statement of faith, to attend preferably twice—every Sunday (unless on holiday, dying or dead), and to dress and behave with decorum "in church." It's what I call the SIGN UP, SHOW UP and DRESS UP approach to membership.

As the charismatic movement grew throughout the 1970s and more churches became open to the gifts of the Holy Spirit expectations shifted somewhat. They were exciting and fruitful times when God did much in our lives and we couldn't spend enough time together. Committed members would gather to attend a long midweek home group for extended worship and prayer, they would be encouraged to contribute prayers or spiritual gifts in the meetings. In time members would also be strongly encouraged to tithe. I label this the STAY UP, PRAY UP and PAY UP expectation.

Since the 1980s and 90s, as society, and so too the church, became more sophisticated much of the spontaneous life of the early charismatic movement became more "processed." Programs, models and courses came aplenty and the simplicity of church life gave way to more complex demands. We had to get our heads round ethical issues (like abortion and debt forgiveness), national campaigns (like March for Jesus and Minus to Plus), new church models (cell, Alpha, G12 and seeker sensitivity) and engage in a constant stream of courses each with its own handbook (*JIM, Forty Days of Purpose, Freedom in Christ. . .*). For many the organizational demand of the projects the church scene constantly churn out, and the expectation to attend the many meetings such complexity produces, caused spiritual exhaustion. You might call it the CHURN OUT and TURN OUT till you BURN OUT.

Some Gain, Too Much Pain

Whilst we can look back and see good fruit in each of the eras referred to above, we need to realize that much of what is at the heart of the Christian life has been obscured as the church has become, for many, an activity treadmill that seems to get quicker and steeper with each passing year.

Charles Swindoll eloquently, but shockingly reveals the effects of giving in to such demands; "Busyness rapes relationships. It substitutes shallow frenzy for deep friendships. It promises satisfying dreams but delivers hollow nightmares. It feeds the ego, but starves the inner man. It fills a calendar or diary but fractures a family. It cultivates a program, but ploughs under priorities."[2]

What's the bottom line then?

Here's a list of what most churches would seem to consider essential components of effective corporate life:
- A well-rehearsed worship band or choir.
- Charitable status (necessitating trustees and full accounts).
- A thoroughly planned and programed weekly service.
- An attractive weekly newsletter.
- A building (owned or rented).
- State of the art PA equipment and instruments.
- OHP / power-point presentations.
- A lively well run Sunday school / kids' club.
- A church office complete with secretary or administrator.
- A full-time Minister (at least one).
- Ideally an employed children's worker or youth pastor.
- An attractive up-to-date website.
- A course for enquirers.
- A course for new members.
- A course for new group leaders.
- At least one social project in the community.
- Committees to care for buildings, employees, activities. . . .

How many of these can be considered as truly essential biblically? None! That's right, none. I'm not suggesting that anything noted above is actually wrong. Just that they are not of the essence and yet they demand 95 percent of leaders' and members' time and money to produce and maintain.

Can the church be the church without such familiar appendages? To answer that, we should look first at Scripture and then some real examples—

I love Acts 2:42–47: "The believers devoted themselves to the apostles' teaching" DISCIPLESHIP, "to the fellowship, to breaking of bread"; FELLOWSHIP, "and to prayer"; WORSHIP, "many wonders and miraculous signs were done. . .they gave to anyone as he had need"; MINISTRY, "and the Lord added to their number daily those who were being saved"; EVANGELISM. Quite simply this is what being the church is all about:

FELLOWSHIP —Being friends, eating together, practical care.

DISCIPLESHIP —Shaping each other's lives by applying God's Word.

WORSHIP —Spontaneously through the Spirit's power and leading.

MINISTRY   —Each person's unique gift expressed in all of life.

EVANGELISM —Sharing the gospel through words, deeds and signs.

This kind of life is natural and spontaneous. There need be no programs to plan, services to outline, few sermons to prepare (much teaching will come by applying God's Word into real situations as they arise). The worship requires no preparation except to open our hearts to the Holy Spirit, and evangelism isn't a committee run event, but an inevitable outcome of living radical Christian lives in close proximity to unsaved family, friends and neighbors.

The result is that rather than becoming a separate compartment of life that takes part in a special building at special times of the week, remote from our families, neighborhoods, working life and leisure, simple church forms relate to all of life.

Rustic Christianity
I'd like to invite you to share in some of the settings where I've seen such simplicity and life combine. Our first port of call is Lytchett Minster

School, Dorset in 1979. It's lunchtime and Linda Smith, much loved RE teacher, is leading the Christian Union. Not a handful of sincere-but-quiet Christian kids trying to survive the secular onslaught, but seventy radiant, praising children crowded into a double classroom to eagerly learn from God's Word. The sense of camaraderie is infectious regardless of age, sex or background. The group has grown from five pioneers a year earlier to seventy regulars who have been saved in a steady stream through their friends' witness.

Not "church" as we would normally define it, but there is more spiritual life and fruit in Room 12 on a Thursday lunch time than most "sanctuaries" have ever known. Not only that, but the five purposes of church are all being fulfilled. Very naturally, fledgling pastoral, evangelistic and teaching gifts are emerging among the students—you see no one has told them they need to be an adult with a theology degree.

Next we're off to northern Uganda. It's late afternoon, the work is done, children back from school and supper is bubbling away. We're in "the Village," as the vast rural areas with scattered homes are known. In the shade of a couple of leafy trees thirty believers gather, smiling and chatting noisily. Babies are crying and gurgling in turn and a gaggle of children start a song that soon spreads through the group. They dance and sing with joy and energy, and then pray short fervent prayers for a neighbor sick with AIDS, for a good harvest, for protection from the rebels now just twenty miles north. Moses, one of the oldest believers, shares the story of Elisha and the siege of Dothan, imparting courage and faith to all. Sick people are prayed for, with expectation of healing, and the families return as the sun sets to enjoy their well earned meal.

A few hours in the plane and we arrive in Sarawak, a tribal area of Malaysian Borneo. Each morning, as the cockerel announces daybreak, the longhouse communal room fills with sleepy chatter as the whole village gathers for mountain tea and prayer. It is forty years since the old one journeyed over the mountain to hear the message of freedom from a Dutch missionary. Old taboos have been broken—no longer do they bury twins alive or burn a home when someone has died in it. Their joy at receiving a free Gospel overflows into sweet song, fervent prayer and vigorous witness to visitors from neighboring villages. Many younger people have learned to read, solely to imbibe the Scriptures both for themselves and to share with the older generation.

Lastly we're guests at Paul and Jayne's house in 1990 South London. Ten people, four nationalities, one passion. It's 8.00 p.m. on Friday and supper is being consumed amongst much laughter and relaxation. It's clear these people love being together. Without a schedule, the chatter turns to a pithy, biblical discussion about the end times and the comments are enlightening and inspiring as the group meditates on the verse "when we see him, then we will be like him." Worship doesn't need announcing, it could barely be held back. Prayers, for unsaved friends, for personal holiness and for earthy practical realities come thick and fast.

Each one of these disparate situations is profoundly simple, yet each one is as brimming with life as an English cottage garden in May.

Resounding to the Echoes of History

I've often envied Doctor Who. Not so much for the space travel—I'm very fond of planet Earth. No it's the Time Travel that interests me. As I have read of bygone moves of God, what is striking is the way God seemingly overlooks large, well-known centers and establishments, choosing instead, small and simple settings in which to pour his life.[3]

Take Duncan Campbell in the 1950s. Destined for high office in the Church of Scotland, his preaching gift drew crowds of five thousand. Yet God called him to a tiny, wind-swept Hebrides village, a career move inspiring derision in many of his associates. Enter God, and observe one of the most powerful revivals the British Isles has known in the past hundred years. If we were God, with our rational minds, I'm sure we'd choose a more central location with good rail and road links!

Wales in 1859 would make an interesting destination too. Another hugely influential grassroots move of God and one in which children play a major part. Whole villagers were saved, with parents— work weary from the mines and groggy from the pubs—being dragged to meetings by their newly saved children. No well organized events here, but numerous small gatherings in scattered settlements led by "ordinary people" and participated in by all present.

We could travel to hundreds of nations over many centuries and see the same pattern at work. Simple, God-initiated movements that grow in number and effect for as long as they resist the temptation to become a human organization and so deflect the glory from God, and transfer their trust to men.

Walk through any town of a reasonable size and you will see monuments to these moves of God; buildings bearing the names "Methodist. . .Pentecostal. . .Salvation Army. . .Apostolic Church" and so on. Many are near empty, still others sold as homes or galleries, and sadly the reality is that for many such groups, their dependence on God was waning even as their buildings were under construction.

Keeping the Fire Alive

What does this mean for us? How can we be those for whom our faith is defined by devoted love and spiritual life rather than the outward trappings of religion?

The critical issue for the western church today is that we are rich in the things that don't matter: Professionalism, real estate, communication technology and sophisticated structures and programs. Yet, too often, we are paupers in spiritual currency of real worth; a humble dependence on God producing an experience of his presence expressed in devoted fellowship, passionate worship and unbridled disciple-making ministry.

It is said that a Bishop once showed the treasures of his church to Thomas Aquinas with the words, "We can no longer say 'silver and gold have I not,'" Thomas replied, "That's true, but neither can we say 'In the name of Jesus Christ of Nazareth rise up and walk.'" The fact is that spiritual vibrancy and human sophistication rarely walk side by side for any distance. We have to make a choice about which one we will keep in step with.

I do not believe that the western church can rediscover vibrant life without jettisoning that which has displaced it. A conscious effort to become simpler and more spontaneous in form and activity is a necessary prerequisite of spiritual life, just as clearing away a concrete driveway is necessary for grass and flowers to grow. Dr. Kriengsak, a Thai church planter once said, "We arrange our church life in such a way that if God does not turn up, we're in trouble!" That is the essence of the true church, where the appearance of life through impressive performance is not enough—it's God we need!

Simple Minds

The wonderful thing is that changing to simpler forms is as one would expect—simple! The challenge is that it takes a radical change of thinking about church. Arnold Bell, a much respected, radically biblical teacher in New Frontiers, identified three enemies of raw New Testament church life,[4] which need to be expunged from our hearts before we can embrace simplicity. They are:
Religiousness: Demanding; "We must do it this particular way."
Traditionalism: Insisting; "We have always done it this way." And Sentimentality: Compelling; "We love doing it this way."

These (and let's be honest we are all vulnerable to them) are the three chief reasons why change to more biblical practice so often is resisted in the church. It brings to mind the visiting preacher who met an elderly life-long member of the chapel. "You must have seen lots of changes in that time" he remarked. "Aye" replied the old man, "And I've opposed every one of them!"

How different from the flexible wine skin required to hold the "new wine" of God's life. How unlike the church we see in the New Testament. How alien to the way God has worked most powerfully the world over for two millennia.

Thinking Kingdom Not Just Church

Meet Phil, thirty-seven years old, an IT engineer and married to Tina with three children under ten. He's been asked to become a cell group leader, but is uncertain about accepting because he is being offered more responsibility at work. The Pastor suggests that work is taking up too much of his time; perhaps he needs to revisit his priorities.

Jenny, a single lady of fifty-three, is an occupational therapist. She sees scores of the most vulnerable members of the community each week. Jenny sees her work as her calling and brings to it a Christ-like compassion. She regularly gets asked about her faith and has the opportunity to share the story of how God changed her life. Yet she has never been asked to share about her work in the church, or been offered prayer. You see, it's not a church activity.

Twenty-eight-year-old Sarah is a full-time Mum who seems to know everyone on the estate. When someone hits a problem it's Sarah they gravitate to for her godly wisdom and calm demeanor. The elders have noticed this and want her to consider joining the pastoral staff. "She's wasted if we don't employ her" one comments. The other mums on the estate might take issue with this view.

We could meet many more with a similar story: Business people, teachers, school governors, homemakers, caregivers, gardeners, students and voluntary charity workers. Not only do they feel that their occupation is second rate compared to church ministry, they are also made to feel that the time they invest in their livelihood or calling competes with the "real ministry" that happens "in church."

All Hands on Deck

It's confession time for me I'm afraid. You see I've been that elder who has resented the busy work lives of gifted people in the church or failed to value their service if its been "outside the church." I've been so desperate at times to keep the "machine" going that I used often to ask too much of people. At the time the church was run on programs, and we "needed" cell group leaders, Alpha coordinators, trustees, youth workers, children's workers and a music group, just for starters.

In a simple grassroots form, the church is a place where people come to be built up and prepared to fulfill God's call on their lives. Yes there might be a minority for whom that call will be played out mainly in church life. But for the vast majority of us the focus of our ministry will be to be salt and light in a dark and decaying world. When we gather as God's people the church will be a place for replenishment, re-orientation and re-energizing for the tasks ahead.

It's worth noting that Scripture records Jesus mentioning the kingdom hundreds of times, but the church—just twice![5] As his followers, we need to reflect his passion. Theologically, the church is the main conduit of God's kingdom. It's the Temple (where he lives), Jesus' Body (doing his work) and the Bride (which he loves eternally). But surely our purpose on earth is not to be preoccupied creating an alternative reality called "church." Rather are we not to engage in the real world, broadcasting the good news of the kingdom by our lives' example and clear gospel sharing?

Make Me a Super Model

In writing this chapter it has been difficult to resist describing in detail what a simple church should look like, thus adding yet another "model" of church, to the bewildering number already on offer. Yet it is important to describe certain characteristics to enable us to picture how the principles might be applied.

Consider the following and, perhaps, use them to evaluate your current church experience. Remember that most churches are pretty institutionalized, but that even one step towards inspirational simple practice is a step in the right direction. In the simple approach—

Worship – will be largely spontaneous and Spirit-led (not front led) with a high level of participation from those present.

Teaching – will be discipleship oriented rather than intellectually orientated, and include discussion and practical application.

Friendship – will be evident through real life interaction between meetings, and the practice of eating together regularly.

Venues – will tend to be local homes wherever possible, with larger buildings rented from time to time as need dictates.

Seating – will reflect family and equality, with no "front" to lead from, but a more circular layout that says "we all contribute here."

Size – will be determined by the need to be intimate, informal and highly participative, with occasional larger gatherings of groups.

Children – will be incorporated in the church's community and meetings, being as involved as adults with all aspects of church life.

Leaders – will be fairly low profile, primarily serving to bring unity, and encourage and equip members to express their unique gift.

Meetings – will be fewer as much of the life of the church takes place naturally and spontaneously as people have more free time.

Organization – will be minimal, negating the need for offices, secretaries, staff, charitable status, committees and high expense.

Atmosphere – will reflect family, with its deep loyalty, security and real relationships rather than mirroring organization or business.

How to Change the World

With simple forms, few buildings and little attention given to public status, won't the church become invisible and impotent? Is it naïve to suggest that such low profile church forms can have the world changing impact that is our purpose and commission? Let's now examine these vital questions biblically, historically and practically.

References

[1] 1 Thessalonians 4:11–12.

[2] *From Killing Giants, Pulling Thorns* by Charles Swindoll.

[3] *The Pilgrim Church* by E.H. Broadbent is the classic historical record of such groups and movements.

[4] *New Frontiers Growing Church Day Conference* in Andover (1996).

[5] Matthew 16:18 and Matthew 18:17.

6

Small Is Beautiful, Big Is Necessary

The Grassroots Impact

Two leaders were chatting at a church growth conference. Mike discovered that Jack had six children "I wish I had six children," said Mike wistfully. "How many do you have then?" his friend enquired. Mike ruefully replied, "Twelve!"[1]

Mustard or Yeast?

In Matthew chapter 13 Jesus tells two parables about the growth of God's kingdom. In one it is likened to a mustard seed that grows until "it is the largest of garden plants." In the other the kingdom is compared to yeast mixed into flour "until it worked through all the dough." It is refreshing to be reminded that the kingdom, expressed primarily through God's church, will be both outstandingly visible and unstoppably penetrating.

In one story, largeness is emphasized, in the other multiplication of tiny life forms is the agent of change. The contrast is interesting when we compare church forms. Should church primarily be a large gathering that meets in a central building, highly visible to the community around? If so, there are major challenges in being truly local, genuinely intimate and effectively participative. Or should the church instead scatter and spread itself throughout an area so its presence is highly localized and relevant through personal contact? If yes, then the issues of impact and numerical growth become vital.

A third question we might ask is "Do we have to choose one or the other?" Can small intimate home-based churches be linked in a meaningful way and, as need determines, meet and work together in larger settings from time to time?

100 million Chinese believers can't be Wong

In 2001 I visited China and met Sister Wong, a twenty-year-old underground church worker. She was in her second year as an evangelist. "How is your work going?" I asked through an interpreter. "Not as good as last year," she began, "I have only planted four house churches this year." (I nodded as if that was exactly the sort of year I was having too, and could sympathize.) I enquired how she went about her work. "I go from house to house offering to pray for the sick and sharing the gospel. Many people do not listen, but God will often heal someone, then we call the neighbors in to hear the gospel and a church starts in that house."

I had the privilege of several days with twenty such courageous believers in a secret training school in central China and the pattern of their vibrant church life became clear. They met in homes. Sometimes fifty or more would squeeze into a basement, more often a dozen or so in a backroom. This gathering was their church. Yet at special times—perhaps when a senior leader or overseas team was visiting, ten or twenty house churches would gather together, as discreetly as possible, in numbers of several hundred.

Far from being ineffective, through these small home-based groups, the Chinese house churches have grown apace for the past two or three decades to number in excess of hundred million believers! This pattern is so instructive to us in the West, as the institutional church mold (traditional denominational or more modern charismatic) becomes increasingly remote from modern culture with its need for a sense of belonging and an experience of community.

Is bigger really better?

There is a common stereotype of small groups of Christians who meet in homes that goes something like this. "An odd bunch with maverick tendencies who lack desire to reach others and who are engrossed with theologically dubious emphases." Many reading this book might carry a prejudice along these lines, which is why this chapter will examine Scripture and Church History to provide an alternative perspective. The contention of this chapter is that smaller groups are actually more conducive to biblical church practice than large ones. First then, let's examine whether there are practical motivations for adopting simpler, more local forms.

Doth everyone hath?

Worship: At the heart of New Testament worship is free, spontaneous expression by every member through the Holy Spirit's prompting.[2] I have observed the following typical patterns in churches with "open worship" over five years of keen observation—

In a gathering of ten people for worship, normally all (100%) will contribute.

In a gathering of twenty people for worship, about fifteen (75%) will contribute.

In a gathering of fifty people for worship, perhaps ten (20%) will contribute.

In a gathering of hundred people for worship, often only five or six (5%) will contribute.

In a gathering of two hundred and fifty people for worship, still around five (2%) will contribute.

In other words the amount of people taking part tends to drop as congregation numbers increase, whilst the proportion of people contributing plummets alarmingly (both because larger meetings always tend to be more strongly "front-led," and because most people are reticent and nervous about speaking out in larger gatherings). Is this a problem anyway? Doesn't it just mean there is more "quality" about the worship if only more gifted people share and the spiritually inept majority remain humbly silent?

As one critic of our open style of worship asserted, "All you get this way is the lowest common denominator." He objected to nervous, vulnerable people stuttering out inelegant prayers and testimonies and prophecies.

My mind turned to the prostitute tearfully pouring perfume on Jesus' feet while the Pharisee despised her; to the breast beating repentance of the tax collector who lacked the "proper religious words" to convey his penitence; and to the God who chooses the "foolish. . .weak. . .lowly. . .and despised"[3] to display his glory. If that's the "lowest common denominator" then it's fine by me!

I remember Agnes, her hands shaking, asking for help to find Psalm 23. Born with learning difficulties, then abused in her home as a child, and later in her work setting, Agnes was a broken woman. Gaunt, subject to manic depression and at times suicidal, she had found hope and peace in the Lord Jesus. As her cracked voice read falteringly through this most familiar of Psalms, the Holy Spirit invaded the meeting. Our calloused hearts softened by compassion for this woman, the words penetrated to our spirits in a way not even the most eloquent of voices could convey.

Yet many will say, "Hang on, I love being with large groups of believers celebrating and singing our hearts out. The unity and power are wonderful." Yes, I agree! My contention is that whilst such gatherings are important for special times (the sense of "event" being enhanced by being less frequent), the biblical norm is for people to worship in groups of a size and style that invites participation from anybody (and hopefully everybody.)

In brief there are several reasons why smaller groups are better as the most regular environment for worship:

1. There is wonderful variety as the Holy Spirit speaks through our different backgrounds, gifts and characters.
2. Without an agenda set by a worship leader or elder, the Holy Spirit—not a human leads and speaks.
3. Biblical worship patterns are followed.
4. We grow more by doing than listening, and learn to hear God more quickly, being in an active rather than a passive mode.
5. We receive the huge encouragement of God using us (even you and me!) to build others up.
6. It really matters whether we do or do not turn up as everyone has a unique part to play.
7. There is little motivation to impress in a small group, so contributions tend to be real and unreligious.
8. It's easier to be truly flexible in a smaller group as there are few logistical matters (time, space, program) to impinge on what God is doing.

The "F" Word

Friendship: (Or, if you prefer, "Fellowship" or even "Food"!) It's pretty obvious, but in a smaller group everyone is known and missed if away for some reason. Friendships that extend beyond the scheduled meetings thrive naturally, especially as with a minimal "program" there is greater time and desire for eating, socializing and working together. But be warned, putting people into small groups doesn't make them devoted friends immediately, anymore than planting a few saplings makes a border. But given time, what develops, like a carefully laid hedge, is strong and intertwined and becomes a place for others to take refuge in.

Ian (the formerly "cynical immigration officer" you may recall from chapter 2) made a comment recently. It was a wistful remark, uttered shyly, following a shared fellowship meal. "As I look around this room I realize that I've come to love every single one of you."

Maggie, a quietly spoken, single lass in our church, collapsed last week. As she awaited her diagnosis in hospital I was amazed at the response of, not just a "few close friends," but the whole church. Genuine grief, heartfelt prayer, visits, cards and gifts. It was a vivid demonstration of how Paul describes the church "Body" in 1 Corinthians 12:26, *If one part suffers, every part suffers with it; if one part is honoured, every part rejoices with it.*

What has seemed to emerge, three or four years after making home church groups the basic unit of the church, is that we have changed. For a start everyone fits. We're all different types of "people-shaped bricks," but like a dry-stone wall, there's a unique place for everyone. Second, it's not an exaggeration to use the word "friendship" to describe the relationships we share. In fact it's the nearest we have ever come to living out the biblical concept of "Koinonia" (fellowship)—a word literally meaning "sharing of life."

As our people have occasionally changed jobs and moved, it has been a concern observing the difficulty they've had integrating into larger churches. Here are typical examples of their responses:

"No one spoke to me for three weeks."

"People who knew each other well talked but ignored me."

"It's not a very friendly environment."

"People just sit there passively waiting for the meeting to start."

Now, I absolutely refuse to believe that people in bigger churches are less loving or friendly than those in smaller communities. I would contend strongly though, that there is an environmental problem with larger gatherings that violates against a sense of belonging and family intimacy by which biblical church is defined.

We need to remember that genuine, sincere love, expressed through warm greeting, devoted friendship and practical interdependence in life, is non optional—in fact it is central to a demonstration of God's kingdom. As Jesus said on his final night with his disciples, "By this all men will know that you are my disciples, . . ." What? could they perform great miracles? Or preach with wisdom and eloquence? Or be influential in society? No ". . .if you love one another." Which leads us to consider. . .

Bringing in the Sheaves

Evangelism: Poor old Philip must have been so narked. There he was running a great revival in Samaria and working on his book "How I took some area for the kingdom," when God sends him off to a desert road (Acts 8). Why? For just one person. Jesus models this disarming one-to-one evangelism style too. Explaining new birth nocturnally to nervous Nicodemus (John 3); risking censure by socializing with sultry Susannah from Sychar (John 4); and getting bent-over Ben of Bethesda back on his feet after thirty-eight years on disability allowance (John 5). We are so used to mass production, mass marketing, and mass media that we can be deluded into thinking "mass evangelism" is the best or only way. Christians sometimes talk yearningly of devising spiritual "combine harvesters" to see people saved in their masses. Whilst we all long for multitudes to be saved, the use of impersonal, synthetic techniques or systems can have little appeal when they fail to reflect God's unique and personal dealings with every one of us.

Critics of home churches would question the ability of small groups to be effective in reaching out, often describing them as a "holy huddle," and certainly some can be introspective. But if they are truly "holy," living distinctive godly lives; and a "huddle," demonstrating warmth and devotion to one another, then that's a potent combination for seeing people saved and added.

Like most churches in our secular, spiritually dense western culture, we find the work of evangelism both hard and slow at times. Yet we have found that a shift to less "public" activities and an emphasis on more personal interaction has helped, not hamstrung, the process of witness. Whilst we used to rejoice at having a good number of guests at Christmas specials and "fun-day" type events, we now realize that the long-term impact on those (often coerced) visitors was minimal. Now if people attend a meeting or social activity it betrays genuine interest. Although we may see fewer "decisions for Christ" than public events produce, it is striking that those who come to faith in smaller settings have usually spent time in close observation of those in the group, and counted the cost of becoming a fellow disciple. For that reason, and because of good, deep friendships, we've found they're much more likely to "stick."

A few years back, I had the interesting task of evaluating the impact of fifteen different churches in our locality. The smallest were 30–50 members, the larger ones numbering 200–300. All were outreach oriented and all enjoying some growth evangelistically, but there was an intriguing trend. The smallest churches—despite having fewer resources for putting on events had almost twice the "lasting fruit" than the larger ones. In churches under hundred, there was one new Christian each year for every nine members (about 11 percent growth), for churches over hundred the impact dropped to one new believer for every sixteen members (about 6 percent). It was a "snap-shot" and we should be wary of statistics. However, those findings suggest to me that smaller churches, who can offer personal relationships and a sense of belonging, have a distinct advantage over larger gatherings, however inspiring their "service" may be.

Hand made or machine produced?

Discipleship: I like "hand-made food." There's something rather unappetizing about mass-produced burgers and chicken portions don't you think? I believe God creates "hand-made followers."

Many of the leaders I have mixed with have used a phrase that makes me cringe in this regard. "We're *putting everyone through. . .* Alpha. . .Membership course. . .Freedom in Christ course. . . ." I know it's only a turn of phrase, but to my ears it sounds too much like a butcher putting so much meat through a sausage machine! God has created us with such individuality, and his way of dealing with us, as with any loving parent, is different for each child. As someone observed, "God loves doing the same thing differently."

I can understand the attraction of a "one size fits all" approach to discipleship. In fact I spent considerable time writing a year's worth of discipleship notes, thinking I could give all our people the same foundation of truth. It was with considerable dismay I discovered that about half the church didn't find the notes at all helpful. Not because they didn't want to learn, they just learned differently.

The reality is that being a disciple is much more about being shaped by people than by books. Think how much our approach to life was molded by seeing how our parents behaved. How they resolved (or didn't resolve) conflicts for example. Or their attitude to money, or work, or the way they communicated. The culmination of Jesus' Great Commission of making disciples across the globe is "teaching them to obey everything I have commanded you."[4] That's a whole lot different from just "teaching them." It involves an exhibition of lifestyle as well as an explanation of lessons. It's why messages on the airwaves, or even Bibles sent to distant nations are not enough to make disciples. It's why the Great Commission starts with the word "Go."

If I asked what five sermons have influenced you most, would you be able to remember that many? How about if I asked about the five people who influenced you most? Not such a problem! Of course teaching, whether we hear it or read it, shapes our thinking and behavior. But the example of people we admire and trust informs our behavior far more potently. Institutional church relies on a weekly lecture to do the job. Biblical church, where lives are on display, and strong relationships permit honest sharing are far more powerful agents of change. If I have demonstrated biblical and godly parenting, and the effect is on display in my children's lives, then, yes, a talk explaining the biblical principles I follow may be of help, but without the example, the talk is mere theory.

Now I realize those who elevate the place of good preaching (as I do) will be choking on their concordances at this point. So I'll draft in the support of Richard Baxter, author of the classic puritan text "The Reformed Pastor." Whilst extolling the need for a commitment to expository preaching, Baxter also lamented how little truth or understanding his listeners imbibed. His solution was to advocate an equal commitment to home visiting for personal ministry of the Word in the form of a discussion to ensure that Scripture was both understood and applied. Discussion based teaching and discipleship is something that Jesus and Paul employed as frequently as a discourse, and we should feel no hesitation in doing likewise.

This is the beauty of discipleship in smaller settings. People can share questions that have arisen from their own Bible reading, or about ethical dilemmas presented to them at work, or even issues in their families and personal lives. Then the Bible can be opened, not for a randomly selected theory lesson, but used like a car manual when your bonnet is up on a cold wet night—seeking with urgency for specific and much needed help!

All the kings horses and all the kings men. . .

Ministry: Have you ever lost the back off a cheap watch, and viewed in horror as countless tiny parts fall on the floor? However hard you attempt to reassemble the fiddly bits, there's always one missing or put back in the wrong place! The watch may look okay from a distance afterwards, but if there's just one part out of place the function will be faulty at best, but probably non-existent.

Likewise, the biblical imperative is that all the people in the church need to fulfill their gift and calling if the group as a whole is to function fully and well. Which part of your body would you be happy to lose? Apart from an appendix (or perhaps a tubby mid-riff) the thought is an alarming one. Even losing a little toe would put us off balance, not to mention the pain. So too we need to embrace church forms that encourage and allow everyone to minister.

It's a no-brainer to ask whether large or small settings facilitate every ministry member best. I suspect that the greatest cause of fall away from church "attendance" is the failure to harness the basic desire every true Christian has to serve and be needed. In the small setting everybody seems to find their niche whether through verbal contributions in meetings, personal ministries such as prayer, wise counsel and hospitality, or kind deeds expressed through visiting, shopping, DIY and a thousand other ways.

Broadly speaking there are two arenas in which our ministry take place: within the context of church life and gatherings, and in the wider setting as witnesses in the world (including family, commerce, work, politics, education and arts). It is this second category that so often is neglected, yet it is the one in which we spend most of our time. In a group of maybe twelve or fifteen people, there is the time to share about the opportunities, victories and challenges we face in God's big wide world, and find ourselves shaped and encouraged to fulfill our ministries in the marketplace, school, hospital or factory. As Paul put it, the ministries in the church are there to *prepare God's people for works of service.*[5]

Having made a case for smaller gatherings being as (or indeed more) suitable for biblical Christianity, we need to turn to the question of global impact. If "this gospel of the kingdom," is to be "preached all over the world as a testimony to all nations"[6] and the task falls squarely on our shoulders as the church, we cannot be satisfied with a few small groups, however high is their "quality."

What was the New Testament experience?

The book of Acts records three striking examples of regional impact issuing from centers of numerical and spiritual strength. Jerusalem, Antioch and Ephesus.

Jerusalem— The "Scatter Gun" example. God allowed a wave of fierce persecution to scatter the believers, numbering probably between five and ten thousand, across the Roman Empire. It seems the membership roll fell by around 99 percent as only the apostles remained in Jerusalem. This unlooked for dispersal, far from sounding a death knell for the infant church, was the harbinger of the gospel leaping across race barriers to the Samaritans (Acts 8), North Africa (Acts 8), Syria (Acts 9) and Gentiles in general (Acts 10).

Believers who had stayed in Jerusalem post-Pentecost, now returned to their places of origin and *preached the word wherever they went* [7] thus planting new churches. It seems they would not have chosen to leave the throng in Jerusalem, but God had other ideas and, not for the last time, allowed persecution to serve his aims.

One of the biggest obstacles to taking new ground is the "huddle instinct" we have as Christians. I suppose it's the downside of loving each other—we are loath to release people to mission. Even "multiplying" a cell group into two new ones often produces mutinous reactions among the ranks! Let alone sending a church planting team further afield.

But as David Devenish observed a few years ago in the church planting manual "Seeds of Change,"[8] when God gathers it's usually in order to scatter. We must resist our natural aversion to God moving people on, even through seemingly negative events like opposition, redundancy or (perish the thought) disagreements. God in his grace has no difficulty in turning such apparent setbacks into opportunities for the seed of the gospel to be scattered to reach more people and more locations.

Antioch—The "Send the Best" example. What a gathering of gift! "There were prophets and teachers: Barnabus, Simeon. . .Lucius . . .Manaen. . .and Saul." It was a dream team. Boy! those guys must have enjoyed being together. They could have spent their lives in Antioch. . .debating together, writing paperback scrolls and hosting (forty-day long) retreats on "seeker-sensitive, fire-catching, new wine-brewing, Jabez-praying church growth." But—you guessed it—God had other ideas. *The Holy Spirit said, "Set apart for me Barnabas and Saul for the work to which I have called them."* [9]

I have often heard church leaders express a desire to develop "an Antioch center" but I'm not sure they know what they are hoping for. They seem to mean "a big, well-known church, with lots of gifted people on the staff who will visit other (smaller) churches to teach and minister." The Antioch Church of the Bible actually gave up their two senior leaders for years in order to plant a string of modest sized churches across the Roman world.

It is becoming increasingly common for churches to publicize their vision as "to become a church of two hundred. . .thousand. . . two thousand" or whatever. At first sight this looks laudable, we all want lots of people saved and added. Sadly not only do such numerical targets quickly become mill-stones around the neck, preventing the church enjoying whatever stage of growth it is currently in, they also challenge a healthy culture of missionary sending whether to domestic church plants or overseas. My concern is what happens when God, as he will, prompts numerous members to share with the elders a sense of call elsewhere. If you are intent on gathering, it's hard to be passionate about sending too! Gathering a large congregation might appeal to human pride or ambition, but striving for size rarely serves the purposes of the Great Commission.

Ephesus—The Training Hub example. Acts 19 records an interesting model which has been little emulated in post-New Testament days, but whose day may soon be coming. Paul "set up shop" in this major commercial center, to teach and train daily, "all the Jews and Greeks who lived in the province of Asia" (Acts 19:10).

For two years this went on resulting in churches being established and resourced right across Asia Minor (including the seven churches John describes Jesus addressing in Revelation 2 and 3). Rather than building up a large central church in Ephesus with plans down the line to plant more into the surrounding towns (a common aspiration for many today), he facilitated people and equipped them to plant "where they lived." I can see this approach having wide application in the days to come.

Imagine several small, very local churches gathering every month or two in a central location for a whole day of fellowship, keynote teaching, encouragement, worship and prophetic prayer. The sense of intimacy and effective discipleship is retained in the weekly home church, whilst the sense of strategic purpose, mission and teamwork across a region is enhanced through the larger gathering.

Let's get historical about it

If the static, central building model of church life doesn't come from the Bible then where does it come from? The gospel and church communities spread like a wind blown bush fire for two centuries without property, social acceptance, human wealth or organization to "help." The turning point was disguised as a blessing, but was in fact a curse that took over a millennium to begin to reverse.

The rot set in when Constantine adopted Christianity as the state religion of the Roman Empire. Prior to that believers had met in homes for the most part and been, at best, socially marginalized, and at worst cruelly persecuted. But they stayed true to the Word.

After Constantine, the edges of worldly power and wealth began to blur with that of the increasingly institutionalized church. To question the church's authority was tantamount to treason and history tells stories of many who paid the ultimate price for calling for a return to true spirituality and the authority of Scripture.

Church buildings and the clergy themselves became symbols of state authority and sometimes the means of taxation and law enforcement too. For twelve hundred years or so this spiritual dark cloud cast its shadow. By AD 1500 there was (for the vast majority of church attendees) no Scripture, no sense of functioning body, no gospel, no believers' baptism and no life in the spirit.

The evidence is that while institutional religion was able to exert political control through spiritual manipulation, it could not win hearts, change minds or save souls. God caused pockets of spiritual life to arise and keep the flame of truth alive through all these dark times, and for the most part these movements met in private homes (usually for fear of oppression).

As the Reformation took hold after 1517, such movements gathered momentum and ultimately took the form of new church forms distinct from the (usually) compromised Catholic communion. In so doing, the erroneous role of the building (as a sacred sanctuary) and the tainted power of the clergy (as an inviolable authority) were broken.

In the centuries since that epoch-marking moment, powerful moves of God have spread and multiplied with increasing regularity. Each started small and met in homes; Anabaptists, Moravians, Methodists, Quakers, Salvation Army, Pentecostals and House Churches to name but some.

Each one had fiery beginnings characterized by repudiation from the religious (and social) establishment. Yet most spread to national and usually international fruitfulness. This "maturity" phase might last ten, twenty or thirty years in which tens of thousands would be saved and powerful works of compassion among the poor would take place. Then, normally within two generations, each movement moved away from its roots to join the establishment, the fiery zeal increasingly "domesticated" and the importance of organization, hierarchy and buildings were elevated to prime place.

In other words, what changed the spiritual landscape through these movements weren't the later advents of buildings and organization, but the multiplication of small dynamic visionary groups in their earlier years. In Methodism, for example it was the "band"—groups of ten disciples and the "class" —slightly larger local communities, all meeting in homes, which transformed the nation. It was much later (after Wesley's death in fact) that a denomination with the chapel buildings we see today was formed.

Those—particularly in the aging New Church movement that is now focusing increasingly on investing in bricks and mortar— who are apt to be dismissive of the emerging home churches, can be confident that God can reach a nation again through the grassroots. After all he's done it often enough before!

God's Nature is seen in God's nature

To conclude this chapter, I'd like to offer a parallel that I have found so helpful in applying God's ways to the church. Creation reflects so much of God's character; his love of variety, the intricate relationships between plants, animals and seasons and the miracle of life implanted into what we call DNA. We do so well (and honor our Creator) by seeking to understand, and cooperate with the life he has already ordained, rather than in our human vanity seeking to invent artificial, lifeless methods to supplant it.

Learning from the Land

Before World War II, the land in Britain had been worked in a remarkably similar way for a thousand years or more. Each community had numerous family-run farms in which a wide variety of crops and animals were raised. Fields were modestly sized meadows with thick hedges and verges in which insects thrived and provided natural pest control (ladybirds eating aphids for example). The land remained fertile through a simple system of rotation; one year root vegetables, the next pasture, the following year brassicas or bean crops and, of course, regular fallow years.

Along comes man with his technology (all brains and no wisdom), greedy for quick, bumper yields. In Britain, 90 percent of hedges were ripped out in the last fifty years of the twentieth century to provide vast fields that could accommodate huge machinery. Variety was lost as the fields were laid down to one preferred cash crop. Soil hates being used for the same thing two years running, so became depleted (requiring artificial fertilizers every year), and pest affected (thus demanding artificial pest poisons). These destroyed the microbes in the soil so it became "dead," and the run off polluted rivers with excessive nitrates producing unnaturally large amount of weed. The food produced, though suspiciously uniform in shape and impressively large in size, contains residues of fertilizer and pesticide causing untold damage to the person eating it.

God is the author of nature

Before you denounce me as a new age green crusader, let us remember that it is God—not the Green Party—who created a wonderfully integrated, varied world where everything has a unique place and purpose as part of the fruitful whole. The same is true of the church. Instead of ripping out the "hedges" of relationships, importing the "combine harvester" of mega publicity campaigns, introducing the "artificial fertilizer" of polished presentations, let us work with the life that God has already put into his church.

We have a Word that is living and active, the Spirit who gives life, and people who in gathering together become living stones. As we allow God's Spirit to lead and work, his word to penetrate our daily lives, and our love for one another to impart life-giving care, encouragement and discipleship, we will see a culture of sustainable, healthy, fruitful church life fit to reach a nation.

So how do we cooperate with that life? We are part of God's creation too with active minds, ideas and preferences. What is our role as stewards of God's life? The following (penultimate) chapter attempts to address some very earthy matters of practice.

References

[1] Borrowed from *Double Cream* by Stephen Gaukroger and Nick Mercer, Monarch books.

[2] See chapter 7, section on worship, where the main NT references are examined.

[3] 1 Corinthians 1:27–28.

[4] Matthew 28:20 (emphasis mine).

[5] Ephesians 4:12.

[6] Matthew 24:14

[7] Acts 8:4.

[8] New Frontiers Church Planting Directory circa 2001.

[9] Acts 13:2.

Where the Seed Hits the Soil
The Grassroots in Practice

Two ministers huddled in the corner of the church hall to talk without being overheard. After a furtive glance one asked, "What's the difference between an organist and a terrorist?" His friend replied, "I don't know." After another nervous glance the answer came, "You can negotiate with a terrorist!"

The Reality Check

Theories are all very well, but life—including church life—is worked out in a nitty-gritty world of financial pressures, PMT, kids overloaded with school work, family illnesses, tensions with neighbors, tiring work schedules, home maintenance and, not least, the struggle against the sinful nature.

Life is just not tidy. Theories can be neat, but reality isn't. That's why I love the New Testament. It doesn't pull any punches or draw the veil over less attractive or appealing aspects of the Christian life. We hear about Paul and Barnabas parting company over a daft disagreement; Peter being a bigoted clot-head towards Gentile

believers and Demas being seduced by the lure of worldly pleasures
—and that's just the leaders! Added to that—drunkenness at Corinth,
laziness at Thessalonica, arrogance at Colosse, legalism in Galatia,
bitchiness at Philippi, heresy at Ephesus and racism in Rome; we see
that vibrant spirituality thrives in the real sin-drenched world.

There is a distinct difference between the responses of
institutional church forms and grassroots gatherings to this dilemma
of forging godly communities in a sin-sick world. The former
separate themselves, physically, socially, culturally and behaviorally
(there are few people more eccentric than religious, super-spiritual
Christians). The latter engage and work out their faith in the middle
of life.

This chapter will, without being prescriptive, attempt to
explore how an inspirational mindset results in church practice that
is quite distinct from traditional patterns, yet closely akin to the
early church. Let's look first at worship, before considering meeting
style, the place of eating together and finally teaching.

Stay on the Altar!

What we mean by worship needs some definition. It's not an
"act," a "service" or a forty minute charismatic knees up before "the
preach"; worship is honoring God in all of life. Paul defined it: *To
offer your bodies* (note: not your "spirits" or "minds" or "hearts") *as
living sacrifices.*[1] Though, as Nick Cuthbert observed,[2] "The problem
with living sacrifices is they keep crawling off the altar!"

John Piper, in his penetrating exposition[3] of Jesus' meeting
with the Samaritan woman recorded in John chapter 4, affirms this
wide-angled-lens view of worship: "The first thing we learn is that
worship has to do with real life. It is not a mythical interlude in a
week of reality. Worship has to do with adultery and hunger and
racial conflict." My less eloquent take on it is:

Seven days of worshiping God

Worship is; Waking up on Monday with a thankful heart *and saying "Good Morning Lord," instead of "Oh Lord, it's morning!"*

Worship is; Giving next door a tomato plant the day after they've moaned about the hedge. . .*and remembering to trim the hedge too.*

Worship is; Vacuuming the house from top to bottom to give your wife a well-deserved rest. . .*and not expecting a medal for it.*

Worship is; Recognizing how many character faults your manager at work is battling with. . .*and choosing not to moan about any of them.*

Worship is; Watching Gardener's World with your wife, when there's Footy on the other side. . .*and not banging on about it all weekend.*

Worship is; Choosing not to ogle at the pretty woman in the short skirt as you drive past her. . .*and not eying her up in the rear-view mirror afterwards.*

Worship is; Even singing on a Sunday with your Christian friends, to sum up perhaps that. . .*all your life belongs to God.*

Cry Freedom!

But, of course, worship is more than lifestyle, it needs to find verbal expression too, both in our personal prayers and praises, and also when we gather as God's family, with mutual love and gratitude to the Lord. And this is where traditions down the ages differ drastically from the Bible's pattern, with catastrophic results.

Let's look at the New Testament record of worship:
A. Powerful not Predictable: Acts 2:4, *All of them were filled with the Holy Spirit and began to speak in other tongues.*
Acts 4:24, *When they heard this, they raised their voices together in prayer.*
Acts 4:31, *After they prayed, the place where they were meeting was shaken. And they were all filled with the Holy Spirit and spoke the word of God boldly.*
Acts 10:44–46, *While Peter was still speaking these words the Holy Spirit came on all who heard the message. . .they heard them speaking in tongues and praising God.*

B. Passionate not Passive: Turning from the narrative of Acts to direct teaching in the Epistles we see that the three classic texts, 1 Corinthians 12–14, Colossians 3:16 and Ephesians 5:18, define the process of worship as a Spirit-prompted, Word-informed, unplanned medley of contributions from anyone and everyone.

Let the word of Christ dwell in you richly as you teach and admonish one another with all wisdom, and as you sing psalms, hymns and spiritual songs with gratitude in your hearts to God [4]

Be filled with the Spirit. Speak to one another with psalms, hymns and spiritual songs. Sing and make music in your heart to the Lord. [5]

When you come together, everyone has a hymn, or a word of instruction, a revelation, a tongue or an interpretation. All of these must be done for the strengthening of the church. [6]

The point here is that true worship needs no human conductor or form to follow. Both in Scripture and throughout the ages, outbreaks of spiritual life have consistently produced patterns of spontaneous, unplanned, unpredictable, vibrant worship full of heartfelt adoration and replete with spiritual gifts.

Such freedom, exalts God and puts every believer on the same plane regardless of status or office, and reflects the New Testament pattern perfectly. But this is too risky for the timorous human heart.

It might get out of control (Whose control? We might wonder). Traditionalists respond with liturgies, conservatives with orders of service and charismatics with worship leaders. Each of these ultimately controls God's people, domesticating their worship with the frequent, dire result of the Holy Spirit being quenched.

Order! Order!

"But!" I hear some cry, "It says 'Let everything be done decently and in order.'"[7] This must be one of the most abused texts in Scripture. Remember Paul wrote this to a bunch of people whose meeting style was based on pagan revelry. They would get drunk, shout one another down as they prophesied, compete for attention with increasingly elaborate outbursts in tongues and brazenly flaunt their sexuality. It was human sin and foolishness that Paul was anxious to curtail, not the freedom of every believer to contribute as God's Spirit inspired. Paul's emphasis here is "Let everything be done!"

C. Participative not Performed: About seven years ago, when this conviction came to us, we dispensed with the role of worship leader. (It was actually me who got sacked as for years I had been leading pre-planned forty-minute praise times with songs in the same key flowing into each other.) As leaders we told the church that we would no longer have worship leading nor a format to our worship, but that everyone was encouraged, even expected, to contribute songs, testimonies, scriptures, prophecies and other spiritual gifts.

Years of passivity don't fade overnight, and at first it could be pretty flat and the main test for the elders was to resist filling in the yawning gaps between contributions. We quickly discovered that sitting in rows facing the "front" reinforced the spectator expectation, so instead we put the chairs in a horseshoe shape with only two or three rows. As musicians we had to learn new skills, such as joining in a song someone in the congregation had started (in whatever key), playing more by ear than written music.

Tidiness had to be sacrificed. Songs might be sung without music, not everyone had the same sensitivity to the Spirit and timing, and the more loquacious people needed guidance to hold back and leave room for shyer people to share. However, the rewards in terms of an increased sense of God's presence, enhanced expectation (what would God do today?), and growing maturity as almost every member learned the joy of hearing God and sharing were richly prized. Far from losing depth or intimacy in worship, we grew to experience the presence and power of God in new and deeper ways.

Don't shoot me I'm only the worship leader!

One thing that has ruffled most feathers in recent years is our questioning the much vaunted, but biblically questionable role of "worship leader." Whilst absent from the New Testament it seems to be the premier position in many of our churches, especially charismatic ones. Some come from the viewpoint: "It's the only practical way to run a meeting well" whilst others elevate gifted musicians to an alarming degree "We need anointed worship leaders to lead us into God's presence."

Let's deal with the practicality argument first. To begin with, it is human presumption to suppose that anyone, other than God, is "running the meeting." Yes, we'd all agree that God has appointed elders to care for and oversee the church. It is healthy and friendly for an elder to welcome and kick proceedings off, pointing people to God and communicating necessary information. But their chief role is to help create a safe, relaxed setting in which everybody feels free to share and God's Spirit himself determines the proceedings.

The response of several of my pastor friends was "That's too risky, what if someone comes out with a bad prophecy or tries to hijack the meeting." The reality is that it's never really happened, but if it did the elders could step in, otherwise they can be quite low profile contributing as anyone else might.

Once or twice over seven years or so a quiet word with someone after the meeting was needed, to encourage him to be more sensitive to the Spirit. Once it was necessary to gently correct a contribution publicly (a last resort as if people think they might be embarrassed by public correction they're much less likely to risk sharing). The real challenge is not people sharing unhelpfully, it's getting them sharing in the first place!

I was sorely vexed recently when I saw an advert for a Worship Leader's Training Day. One seminar was entitled, "How to encourage participation without it becoming a free-for-all." WHAT? GOD HAS MADE IT A FREE FOR ALL!

Biblically it is the Body, not the leaders alone (let alone "worship leaders"), through whom the Holy Spirit moves to direct, encourage, glorify God and release his power. Most meeting set ups resemble a concert rather than a participating body, no wonder gifts of the Spirit are becoming rare as hen's teeth in many places, as people receive the subliminal message "you are here to watch."

Own up. Who ripped the curtain?

The other (inadvertently heretical), preconception, is betrayed by a phrase commonly uttered by leaders and members alike. "It's so good to have anointed worship leaders to bring us into the presence of God." In chapter 4 we observed how many leadership forms encroach on God's sovereign territory, here's two more. One concerns use of the word "anointed." In the New Testament it is reserved for Jesus alone,[8] "Christ" (Greek) and "Messiah" (Aramaic) meaning literally "The Anointed One." (By the way, alternative New Testament language describes people as gifted or full of the Spirit, both terms that look beyond the human recipient to God himself).

Second, only one Person can, and has led us into the presence of God:

> Therefore, brothers, since we have confidence to enter the Most Holy Place by the blood of Jesus, by a new and living way opened for us through the curtain, that is, his body. . .let us draw near to God with a sincere heart in full assurance of faith.[9]

Queuing up at the labor exchange

So are musicians and "worship leaders" redundant? No indeed, (though the latter will need to be redeployed). One might ask what biblical gift, worship musicians are fulfilling, if "worship leading" is felt to be an unhelpful description. My personal conviction is that musicians should see themselves as expressing the gift of encouragement[10]; serving, inspiring and enabling the people of God in their worship. We could even start calling them "worship encouragers" to divert the focus from individuals to the Body.

The Bible signifies praise in song and with a vast array of instruments. "Praise him on the trumpet. . .harp and lyre. . .with tambourine and dancing. . .with the strings and flute. . .with the clash of cymbals."[11]

With informal, highly participative forms of church gathering, the musicians' role is no less important, just different. They can serve and enable the Body by:

- Writing songs (it's great when local groups sing "home-grown songs." rather than reworking the current Christian "top ten").
- Teaching songs, thus keeping the church's repertoire fresh.
- Playing songs that non-musical people request.
- Accompanying songs members have begun by "singing out."
- Performing presentation songs for ministry or evangelism.
- Inspiring and teaching many more people to play instruments!

Where have all the strummers gone?

This last point is a passion of mine. In the 1970s, as God's Spirit moved in renewal it was common for more than half of the people in a home gathering to be strumming guitars (adorned with *Smile Jesus Loves You*, stickers!). Songs were beautifully simple, so three chords were generally sufficient, and competence was within the reach of the many. There was a great "folk" feel that encouraged everyone to have a go both in playing and song writing.

Gradually, over the ensuing twenty years, worship music became "professional." Songwriters, led by Graham Kendrick, incorporated complex melodies, tempos and chord progressions and only the more gifted or trained musicians could keep pace. Whilst great tunesmiths like Kendrick, David Fellingham, Dave Bilborough and more latterly Stuart Townend and Matt Redman, have contributed many wonderful songs and recorded numerous fantastic CDs, there has been a downside too. There is a barrier of musical elitism.

As I have tried to encourage many to take up the guitar to play for worship (we needed more musicians as new home churches were formed), the response was often "I could never play like so-and-so" (naming an accomplished musician in the church). So they ended up not playing at all. Our response has been to encourage a revival of simpler songs in worship, with simple repeating chord patterns that can be learned easily and sung without the need for music books, and to invest time teaching groups of budding guitarists.

O(h) H(oly) P(rojector)

But it isn't only the style of leadership that needs reviewing if we are to achieve greater participation in worship; the layout has a massive impact too. My former lecturer,[12] Arnold Bell tells of an incident at a funeral held in their informally laid out building: The pallbearers, accustomed to bowing towards the altar, arose having laid down the coffin, and with a growing sense of panic looked around to see just people in a circle of chairs. It was with great relief that one of them spotted the overhead projector towards which they gratefully bowed and genuflected!

It's amusing but also cautionary because almost every meeting place I have been in seems to have a "substitute altar" of some kind. Whether a carved communion table, projection screen or even a plastic school table, we seem to want to look at and sing to anything instead of one another.

There is a beauty about sitting in a circle together—whether a single arc in a small group, or several concentric circles in a larger gathering and worshiping God "in the midst." There's something rather disconcerting about staring at the backs of rows of people with their arms raised up towards the worship band!

When newer churches (by that I mean eighteenth century non-conformist chapels onwards) lay out their chairs or pews "facing the front" they are, ironically, "conforming" to the style adopted by the Roman State Church of the third and fourth centuries. If we realize that the "altar" pattern is one carried over from the Old Covenant, when a human priest was necessary to stand between God and the people, it will help us to see how such a pattern is ill-fitting today now Jesus has stood "in the gap" and made a way for us all to enjoy God's presence.

Atmospheric Conditions

Meeting layout is just one example of what shapes the vital, but hard to define, matter of church atmosphere or culture. It would be interesting to ask our congregations what three words they would apply to the atmosphere in the meetings. Would it be, friendly —welcoming—relaxed—inclusive—free—? Or perhaps, serious—formal—structured—impersonal. . . ?

"Culture" is far more important than mission statements and even doctrinal statements in determining how people behave in the meeting setting. The danger with more institutional settings is that people go into a "meeting mode." They can be chatty and friendly before and after the meeting, but during it, become unnaturally sombre and reserved, adopting a poise of rigid formality or soupy spirituality, even succumbing to a state of glazed-eye passivity.

In 2006, I visited a beautiful church in Albania and was deeply impressed by the warmth of their friendships towards one another. As we chatted outside the hall they were to meet in, the early evening air echoed with their laughter and bonhomie. Five minutes later and a eerie transmogrification had taken place as they filed into their rows for the meeting. Silence descended like a pall as these good people sat with knitted brows pensively listening to their leader's exhortations, then mournfully sung what I assume were praise songs, but which sounded more like funeral dirges.

Why did they behave in such a way? Not because of any lack of joy in their relationship with God—in informal settings they overflowed with life—it was purely a product of how they had always seen people behave in meetings, modeled, alas, by English missionaries.

Cultural Revolution

How do we influence the culture or ethos of our gatherings to reflect what we are, a God-filled, Spirit-led family? Here are some pointers which can apply to home meetings as well as larger gatherings:

• Lead in a low-key way that encourages participation from all.
• Embrace spontaneity and dispense with a program.
• Lay the chairs out in the most circular pattern possible.
• Get children involved as they behave freely and naturally.
• Start with tea and coffee and let the buzz flow into worship.
• Exhibit real emotions and avoid spiritual language or poise.
• Enjoy God's wonderful gift of humor, it opens our hearts.

Grub's Up

As useful as this list might be, there's a part of church culture that can't be created by meeting dynamics, but only by genuine friendships and time together—we might call it community. My brother once gave our parents a plaque that read, "The family that prays together stays together." I've adapted it to apply to the church family; it goes, "The church that can munch becomes a close bunch." No, it's not very good but you get the point!

As we observed in chapter 5, life is hectic, but we all need to eat, and eating together is a powerful way to say, "we accept each other, we are family, we have a common bond." (Incidentally that is why eating with someone was so significant in Scripture. It explains Paul's castigation of Peter not eating with Gentiles because, by declining, Peter was rejecting them. It was also the reason that church discipline of an unrepentant member led to the instruction "with such a man do not even eat."[13])

Eating together was in the genes of the early church from the outset, not just occasionally either, as they "they devoted themselves to. . .breaking of bread." As well as gathering in the Temple courts on a daily basis they continued their fellowship by repairing to various houses for refreshment; "They broke bread in their homes with glad and sincere hearts."

I like those two words—glad and sincere. Gladness conveys warmth, humor, smiles and joy. Sincere, from the Latin meaning "without wax," was a guarantee sculptors used to validate that "this is genuine, what you see is what you get." They are the antithesis of formal church life, so often marked by somberness and unreality.

Dining Together

The late Simon Pettit, a much respected and sadly missed apostolic figure once remarked: "We've learned how to fast and pray together, it's time we learned again how to eat together."[14] How true that is.

I'd venture to suggest that nothing (including prayer and teaching) has deepened our sense of community more than eating together on at least a weekly basis.

Our church is a funny bunch. Being so different in personality, stage of life (remember it's all age with young children and teens as part of the mix), occupation and background. Yet when we eat together potential barriers evaporate. The first thing you notice if you look around is the gladness. As people cradle plates on their knees and chat to those around them you can see from their smiles and laughter that they're pleased to be there and yes—they're having fun. The second thing that becomes apparent (as you ear-wig a few conversations) is the sincerity as people share candidly about their lives; family issues, work situations, health matters, household headaches, shopping expeditions. . .you name it.

Without any formal organization, needs get met. Lifts to appointments are offered and accepted. Thoughtful advice is sensitively proffered and welcomed. DIY help is promised and social activities arranged. A dozen pastoral needs are met (without the Pastor's "help") and all over a plate of spaghetti Bolognese!

What's the recipe?

It's tempting to make this style of meeting sound perfect, but of course we've made many mistakes over the years, and here are some of what we've learned. . .

Time: People eat at different times. Younger children often want something soon after five, some folk aren't in from work till seven. We've found that an hour's "window" say 5.30 p.m–6.30 p.m works well (it suits over 90 percent of the group), and that anyone coming later has a meal set aside that they can eat as the meeting continues.

Venues: Weekly meals for 15–20 people take time and money, and it's good to share the hosting around. Hosting once a month is reasonable for many, but if 6–8 folk are willing to share the hospitality that's better still.

Ethos: Because it's natural to want to host really well, meals tend to get more and more elaborate as time goes on ("Marjorie did a nice dessert last week, I'd better do one too") so simplicity needs to be regularly encouraged and modeled—especially by the leaders. A simple nourishing meal, being easy to serve and keep warm, then some fruit, is ideal and what many would normally have at home.

Meals: Fork food is great, especially when it's a lap meal. Our favorite meals (for simplicity of cooking and ease of eating) are:
Pasta Bolognese (with pasta twists rather than spaghetti).
Chilli con carne with rice (not too hot).
Mexican bean feast with bread or pasta.
Home made soup with crusty bread.
Sausage casserole.
Pizzas.
Jacket potatoes with tuna and grated cheese.

Seating: Whilst sitting round a table might suit a smaller gathering, the fact that people are arriving at different times, and it's hard to be sure of the exact number has meant that eating on laps (or lap trays) seems most appropriate. Where there are young children (or elderly) for whom that might be difficult, it's good to have a small table one end of the room where a few can sit more easily.

Breaking bread: We've found these informal meals a great setting in which to "break bread." Jesus' inauguration of communion (or "the Lord's Supper" or "the Eucharist" depending on your background) was in the context of a real meal. When divorced from the meal setting, what should be a joyful, faith-imparting event becomes solemn and religious.

As a small child I was ill at ease in partaking in what seemed a mystical, even eerie ritual. Poker faced stewards, moving in perfect synchronization on either side of the chapel, passing cubes of bread and a sweet syrupy wine substitute in hushed silence. As Wolfgang Simpson in his thought-provoking treatise, "Houses That Change the World" observes: "Church tradition has managed to celebrate the Lord's Supper in a homeopathic and deeply religious form, characteristically with a few drops of wine, a tasteless cookie and a sad face. However the Lord's Supper was actually more a substantial supper with a symbolic meaning. . .God is restoring eating, back into our meeting."[15]

The meeting: We need to get rid of the false divide between "social" and "spiritual" aspects of our meeting. The meeting starts, not when the first song is sung, but when the first person arrives for the meal. We have found there is a natural flow from informal fellowship and chat to prayer, worship, or teaching.

It's all-age, so before the children disappear to play or do homework, it's great to draw them into the main focus of the evening. Then, while older children will tend to stay in for the duration of the meeting, it's great to be flexible enough not to expect six or seven year olds to engage in the whole meeting, and give them the freedom to play for some of the time.

Activities: The biggest challenge for churches is to avoid the "program trap." Somehow we feel insecure if there is not a ten- week Bible study series planned or a six-week series of prayer evenings. God loves it when we meet with him without our predetermined agenda and allow him to lead. As this happens, it's amazing what a great variety of ministry is released for example:

On a summer's evening, the group might go down to the park, joining in a few locals with a game of rounders, and inviting them to next week's meal.

A debate sparked by a news item about "Gay Marriage," prompts the group to find enlightenment in the Scriptures.

A member's family crisis provokes shared sorrow, heartfelt prayer and wise advice.

Questions about spiritual gifts, draw out some teaching and testimony about baptism in the Holy Spirit and result in a number of newer folk being prayed for and receiving.

Neighbors are invited to a barbeque evening at which three of the group share brief testimonies.

A work party to help decorate a disabled member's flat follows the shared supper.

It's interesting to note that all the elements we try to include through rigid programs, happen naturally and appropriately as we meet simply with God; evangelism, discipleship, worship, fellowship and ministry.

Pass the de-greecer

Finally, how do we approach the vital area of teaching and discipleship. The quick answer is by becoming more Hebrew and less Greek! Hebrew thinking is holistic—God is in all of life and there is no sacred/secular divide. The Greek mindset (shaped by something called platonic dualism) sees the spiritual and academic as elevated and the material as common and of little value. I love the instruction in Deuteronomy 6:7–8:

> Impress them (God's laws) on your children. Talk about them when you sit at home and when you walk along the road, when you lie down and when you get up. Tie them as symbols on your hands and bind them on your foreheads.

That's the way God's Word shapes our lives, as we discuss and apply it to everyday matters, not keeping it to an hour on a Sunday morning.

The Pharisees of Jesus' day applied this command in a fatuous display. of piety, literally tying boxes called phylacteries to their hands and heads, not realizing that the symbolism is that God's Word should inform all that we do with our hands (give or take, work or steal, strike or protect) and think in our heads (love or hate, lust or respect, fear or trust). Could it be that we have been guilty of locking God's Word away in phylacteries of our own; the Sunday meeting perhaps, or even our daily quiet time?

Another brick in the wall

What has this to do with teaching? First, that Bible teaching is too often reserved for a special time each week (Sunday morning), and is separated from the rest of life, in which the Scriptures are barely opened and rarely applied. Second, the style of preaching tends to be a lecture, communicating concepts and ideas, rather than the more pictorial and interactive style which Jesus modeled.

When questioning the place of preaching in the church there are those who will passionately defend the weekly place of detailed expository preaching. It's important to be clear that by embracing the Word of God in a less formal, but more pertinent way, its relevance and power in our lives are enhanced, not depleted. There is always a place for gifted Bible teachers to be given the floor (and our attention) for discourses of keynote importance. But, I would contend, to be effective in shaping our lives such teaching needs to be partnered with three other styles of teaching and discipleship.

A) The word of instruction: One of the spiritual gifts described in 1 Corinthians 14:26 is the "word of instruction," something we rarely hear done in the context of open worship. This is distinct from someone just reading a passage that God has prompted and sitting down again. It is the practice of reading, perhaps just one verse, and under the Spirit's leading, explaining and applying it in a pithy, relevant way. It is arguable that these kinds of contributions, from several members rather than a single preacher, were the norms in New Testament days. Whether that was the case or not, we need more insightful exhortations of this kind, especially as they are one of the elements that Paul asserts, *". . .must be done for the strengthening of the church."*[16]

B) Teaching into life: Jesus' teaching on divorce wasn't a prepared study, it was the answer to a question; *"Is it lawful for a man to divorce his wife for any and every reason?"*[17] Moments later his instructions about the value of children were provoked, not by a seminar title, but by commenting on his disciples' poor behavior. In fact, the majority of Jesus' teachings as recorded in the Gospels were inspired by these two impulses, questions and events.

We too should see that the most potent, life-enhancing teaching can be done—not as a remote seminar, but as a response to life's dilemmas and traumas; a rebellious teen, annoying neighbors, debt problems, fears about terrorism, persecution at work or attitudes to growing older. All that is needed is an environment, small enough and friendly enough where such realities can be aired with confidence.

C) Interactive teaching in small groups: As well as more spontaneous instructions, there is a place to teach in a more systematic way. Paul told the Ephesians, *"For I have not hesitated to proclaim to you the whole will of God"*[18] and instructed Timothy, *What you have heard from me, keep as the pattern of sound teaching.*[19] Such teaching might be a set-piece discourse, especially in a larger setting, but to be worked into our lives, there also needs to be regular interactive instruction so that truth is fully understood and applied.

In the home church setting, such teaching, remembering it is of all age, tends to have the following characteristics:

- Shorter (10–15 minutes)
- Vivid and visual, (plenty of objects and action)
- Child inclusive (though not child centered)
- Interactive and participative
- Flexible according to need or response, and
- Always containing practical life application.

It's amazing how much you can say in a quarter of an hour, that's about the length of the Sermon on the Mount and the Epistle of James, so short doesn't mean lightweight! In fact one could ask, if you can't say it in fifteen minutes, are you going to be able to say it at all?

The other releasing aspect of this kind of teaching is that lot more people do it. In our church over half the members (male and female, young and old) give informal talks, bringing wonderful variety and insight from different perspectives. Whilst authoritative doctrinal teaching is reserved for gifted teachers, this kind of practical instruction is open to all and we learn so much about God and each other through sharing such riches.

Simply Family
Describing a fresh approach to worship, teaching, meeting style and church culture can sound much more complex than it is. All that has gone before in this chapter can be summarized in the maxim, "Think Simple, Think Family." As we do this, the beautiful and natural qualities of love, acceptance, value, reality and vibrant life will inevitably inhabit all we are and all we do.

A woman's prerogative?
No, we all need to change our mind sometimes. It's not easy though to look at things differently when we've been programed by a rational culture and an institutional church pattern. Praise

the Lord that one of the fruits of giving ourselves to him, being open to his Word and filled by his Spirit is that we are *transformed by the renewing of our mind.*[20]

A young Christian lad was talking to his anxious mother who said, "I'm worried you'll get brainwashed. His reply was, "If you knew what my brain was like you'd agree it needed washing!" If we can somehow "wash" from our minds the expectations that come from our church experience, contaminated as it is by human "additives," and read the New Testament afresh, our practice might soon become very different.

The final chapter will offer compelling reasons why, at this point in world history, a new wave of grassroots churches are so desperately needed and are to be welcomed, not feared. Finally, space will be given to review how the principles offered in this book can be applied to believers and churches in diverse situations.

References

[1] Romans 12:1.

[2] An off the cuff remark made during a lecture at Roffey Place in 1984.

[3] Desiring God by John Piper, chapter 3 "Worship," published by IVP.

[4] Colossians 3:16 (my emphasis).

[5] Ephesians 5: 18b – 19 (my emphasis).

[6] 1 Corinthians 14: 26, (my emphasis).

[7] 1 Corinthians 14: 40.

[8] The only exceptions being the plural uses in 2 Corinthians 1:21, and 1 John 2:20 and 27 where the term is applied to the corporate Body of Christ. Never is it used of an individual.

[9]Hebrews 10:19–22.

[10] Romans 12:7

[11]Psalm 150:3–5.

[12]Arnold was, for many years, senior lecturer and director of the excellent "Equipped for Ministry" leaders training course that I was privileged to attend in 1998–2000.

[13]I Corinthians 5:11.

[14]From a Stoneleigh Bible Week seminar circa 1996.

[15]*Houses That Change the World* by Wolfgang Simpson, OM publishing, 1998.

[16]1 Corinthians 14:26.

[17]Matthew 19:3.

[18]Acts 20:27.

[19]2 Timothy 1:13.

[20]Romans 12:2.

8

Digging for Victory
The Grassroots Application

A lone traveler had fallen over a cliff at night and just managed to grab hold of a bush near the top. As he hung there over the black precipice he yelled, "Is anybody down there?" To his surprise a voice replied, "Yes! I am God, let go of the bush, I will catch you safely." There was a long pause before the traveler called again, "Is anybody else down there?!"

The Safety Net

Why are traditions so appealing? Mainly, I think, because they make us feel safe. In the *Lion, the Witch and the Wardrobe,*[1] as Lucy hears how awesome is the lion called Aslan, she asks Mr. Beaver "Then he isn't safe?" Lucy receives the disarming reply, "Safe?. . .who said anything about being safe? Course he's not safe. But he's good. He's the King I tell you." If we are to abandon ourselves to the flexibility of following the Spirit's leading, and a radical response to applying God's sharp, uncompromising Word, we must begin to value spiritual adventure above risk-free religion.

135

The world accepts tame piety, although it despises it too, but reserves all its vitriol and bile for those who deign to follow Jesus in radical discipleship. To a godless society, authentic Christianity will always appear intolerant, offensive, extreme and out of kilter. Jesus told Nicodemus *"Everyone who does evil hates the light, and will not come into the light for fear that his deeds will be exposed."* [2] The kind of church that carries God's presence and proclaims his Word is on collision course with secular society however "civilized" it purports to be. A church that does not provoke some kind of negative reaction from a sinful culture is just not doing its job.

The Tug of War

The church has ever been pulled in two directions: to become more Christlike, or to align itself with the world. The contention of this book is that to rediscover spiritual vitality, we need to discard the heavy cloak of convention that hampers our true freedom and disguises our identity. This is not the work of a moment, nor is it a one-time-only action. Traditionalism always presses on the Spirit-filled church trying to force it into a world shaped mold.

How should we respond? The answer will differ for each of us, but rather than see it as a stark choice between two poles, it is helpful to see ourselves, as it were, traveling on a railway line between two stations, "Institutionalism" and "Inspirational Life." The vital questions are: "Which way are we facing?" and, "Are we moving?"

If we see ourselves on a continuum rather than on one side or another it will help us in two ways: a) To avoid spiritual pride and condemnation of certain traditions or church groupings, and b) To discern how, in our personal walk with God as well as our church setting, we can make steady, significant changes to become more inspirational and less hidebound by human tradition and control.

Changing Rooms

There's an amusing series of jokes on the lines of:"How many charismatics does it take to change a light bulb?" (Answer: Four, one to unscrew it, and three to share the experience!) Another goes,"How many Brethren does it take to change a light-bulb?" (Answer: What do you mean "change"?) Given Christian intransigence, there's no reason why the Brethren should be singled out for such stereotyping. The point is we all need good reason to face the inevitable discomfort and effort required to change.

In these crucial last days, there are three compelling reasons why as individual believers and church communities we need to embrace change to simpler, more dynamic and intimate gatherings:

Persecution issues: A church that can survive outside the law.

Penetration issues: A church that reaches all parts of society.

Personhood issues: A church that embraces all in its family.

Love–Hate Relationship

A) Persecution: The more we love God, the more the world hates us. It's a simple but uncomfortable equation. In Britain and other western nations, the concept of persecution is no longer a distant threat, something associated with living in Communist China or Islamic Iran. As these words are being written, believers in an English west country university are being told that they cannot meet as a Christian union on campus. The university objects both to membership being reserved for Christians only, and the biblical stance the group takes to the homosexuality question.

At national level, Anglican and Catholic adoption agencies are being given the stark choice to place children, against their principles, with same sex couples, or to face prosecution or even closure under so called "equality" laws. Additionally, many commentators today, both political and Christian, predict a growing threat of attack from

Muslim extremists, particularly in those inner city boroughs where adherents of Islam form the majority of the population.

It would not be apocalyptic (or even apoplectic!) scare mongering to forecast that in just a few years, biblical churches will not be allowed to enjoy charitable status, hire public buildings such as schools and town halls, openly evangelize or even act as employers.

There are three options of how to respond to the reality of believers being increasingly marginalized by the press, intimidated by opponents and disenfranchised by the law. Ignore, fight or rejoice.

Head in the sand, or sword in our hands?

Ignoring opposition is a position one can adopt now, but not necessarily for much longer. How about fighting discrimination then? Some Christian groups, such as evangelical lobby Faithworks as well as individual groups that are targeted, assert their right to social acceptance. They argue that British and European cultures are built on Christian values, and contend that society owes us a debt for introducing healthcare, education and social reform. As such, they maintain, Christians should be able to access public funding, hire public facilities and fulfill their role in society even if some of their beliefs are at odds with secular humanism.

Whilst such bullishness is admirable and understandable, history shows that fighting for our rights can be a huge distraction from our central calls to communicate the gospel and be the people of God. It is also built on a faulty preconception that vibrant spirituality can co-exist peacefully with a world system that, at its heart, opposes God worship violently. The New Testament affirms that the only two reasonable responses to uncompromising gospel preaching are persecution or conversion, nowhere do we see luke-warm tolerance.

It's fascinating to observe how the early church endured the white-hot fury of the Jewish establishment as well as the arrogant cruelty of Roman rule. They refused to be silenced (Acts 4:19), prayed for boldness (Acts 4:29), risked their lives (Acts 5:33), honored martyrdom (Acts 7:59) and used the effects of persecution to spread the Word more widely (Acts 8:4). Never it seems did they whine about their hardships. Having just seen their Master and Lord hounded to death, it seemed only natural that rejection and vilification would be their lot. On the contrary after a flogging. . . *the apostles left the Sanhedrin, rejoicing because they had been counted worthy of suffering for the Name.*[3]

Rejoice in the Lord within reason

Frank Gamble, a wonderful pastor and preacher who died in his fifties after years of agonizing illness, used to preach a great message on rejoicing under trial. He pretended to be on the mobile phone to Paul. Frank's half of the conversation was hilarious as he responded to "Paul" talking about his flogging in Philippi. "I see, you were in prison and flogged. . .right. . .and in the night you were 'stinging'? . . .WHAT? You were SINGING!. . .I bet that brought the house down."

Frank cleverly communicated what Jesus made crystal clear two millennia earlier *"Blessed are you when people insult you, persecute you and falsely say all kinds of evil against you because of me. Rejoice and be glad, because great is your reward in heaven."*[4]

Spiritual Guerrilla War

What has this to do with church forms? Firstly, that the institutional church will be the first to feel the heat of opposition in these last days. Their buildings advertise their existence, their bank accounts can be frozen and their membership rolls investigated. They will be faced with the hard choice of being faithful to God's Word or letting go of much that is held dear in terms of social acceptance, historic veneration, property, status and wealth.

Second, what believers from first century Palestine to twenty-first century Pakistan have shown, is that home churches survive and thrive under the fiercest opposition. There is a classic tale of state soldiers invading a meeting and demanding, "If you're not a believer leave now, we will shoot everyone who remains." Once a few half-hearted attendees have hastily departed, the soldiers lay down their guns and say, "we wanted to be sure there were no informants here, tell us how we can be saved." Whether apocryphal or not such accounts communicate a vital truth: that the persecuted church is a dedicated one where believers have counted the cost, turned their backs on worldly "success" and in trusting God fully, are fruitful.

Having met a few survivors of Soviet and Chinese persecution and seen firsthand the evidence of crippling torture, health destroying hard labor and life robbing internment, I would be a fool to hope for persecution. Yet, if we take Scripture seriously, it will come whether we would wish for it or not. Timothy heard it from his stone and whip scarred tutor *But mark this: There will be terrible times in the last days,*[5] Paul then adding, *In fact, everyone who wants to live a godly life in Christ Jesus will be persecuted.*

In adopting the simple forms and radical disciple lifestyle advocated in these pages, we will be preparing both spiritually and practically for a time that is coming on soon when Christians and their message will be no longer enjoying acceptance by society.

B) Penetration issues: The following "Types" represent thousands who are out of reach of organized church.

Nick is fifteen and lives with his Mum. Dad left when he was five and he's been batted between parents like a ping-pong ball ever since. His mates are similarly alienated, enjoy a fight and a spliff and speak a language pretty much their own. The gulf between Nick's gang and formal church life is all but impassable.

Wesley is a twenty-year-old British Caribbean. His life consists of casual work and casual relationships. He's having lots of "fun" he thinks, and wouldn't go near a church because "it is so boring, and is all a load of 'Thou shalt nots.'"

Tony and Rose are retired and approaching seventy. Whilst they put "Church of England" on their hospital forms, neither darkens the door of the village church except for baptisms, marriages and funerals, or as they call it, "Hatch, Match and Dispatch." They have never really heard the gospel, and early memories of the second World War cause them to question the existence of a loving God.

Fiona is a nurse aged thirty, who thinks, "There must be something out there." Yet occasional visits to church have not answered her need to find out about God. She finds the services okay and the people quite friendly, but the language is over her head. Besides, everyone looks and dresses so differently from her, she wouldn't fit in.

"Sorry I don't understand, I can't speak Christianese"

As Christians we're apt to moan about how "dark" our nation is and how spiritually unresponsive people are. Could it be that the problem is more ours? That what people are apathetic or negative about is an institutional church that communicates impersonally through roadside posters, fliers through letterboxes and adverts in the local rag? Also, that they're turned off by archaic buildings and language, not to mention ridiculous ecclesiastical attire. What will effectively reach every pocket of society is not a high profile mega church, a really clever publicity campaign, or a powerful super-evangelist. . . , but seeing the reality of God in someone they know. Then, through that person, meeting a community of believers who will welcome them in to see the reality of following God first hand.

In a way, Nick, Wesley, Fiona, Tony and Rose each represents an "unreached people group." Almost as surely as the Tuareg people of Mali or the Kayastha tribe of India, people in the "post Christian"

West need to be reached by small, localized and dedicated mission teams. . .we might call them home churches.

Nick and Wesley's only chance of hearing the gospel any time soon is at their local burger bar where a small bunch of Christians hang out for fellowship and to share their faith. For Fiona, a lunchtime fellowship in her hospital might become "church" as two of her colleagues have been asking her along. Tony and Rose don't know it yet, but a couple in their bowls club are planning to have them round for lunch in the hope of a chance to share their testimonies and maybe invite them to small group of believers that meet each week for lunch in their home.

None of these groups are any great shakes on their own, but small church groups such as these are being the salt and light we are called to be, dispelling the darkness in many remote corners and mingling with every part of society to bring the good taste of the gospel to all. They are actively fulfilling the Great Commission and effectively expressing each aspect of the church's function. It is multiplication of these kinds of flexible, highly localized and intimate church gatherings that will ensure every person has an opportunity to both hear the gospel in a relevant way, and see its power in the lives of others.

Let's get personal
C) **Personhood issues:** You can't have a relationship with an organization, only with other people. Probably the biggest group of Christians in the West today are not Anglican, Methodist, Catholic or New Church, they are the "out of churchers." People who have a genuine faith, but who have hit against the wall of formality, structure, organization or legalism in church life and felt unable to fit in. Some have given up church after years of trying, and many carry huge guilt through feeling the problem is theirs alone.

For so many of these good folk, it has not been essential issues

of faith and relationship with God that have caused their alienation. Rather they have been damaged by experiences such as:
• Never having their gift or contribution valued and used.
• Receiving heavy-handed correction or pressure to conform.
• Feeling they can't live up to the "Holy" image others convey.
• Being made to consistently feel guilty and a failure.
• Finding the spiritual atmosphere dull or unreal.
• Suffering alone because others are oblivious of their needs.
• Never being befriended or feeling accepted.
• Disillusionment when promised "vision" fails to materialize.

Steve Goss in his helpful material entitled *Freedom in Christ* has summarized our three basic needs as significance (that we matter and have a part to play), security (that we will be cared for) and acceptance (that we're loved). All these needs are powerfully met in a healthy relationship with God, but it is vital that God's family fulfills them too if we are to reflect his glory and nature.

Whilst most churches of whatever size or tradition attempt to be friendly and caring, their very structure violates against it. The huge number of once keen church members who have haemorrhaged from the church in the past two decades is evidence enough that we need a return to grassroots church forms where every person belongs, is cared for as a friend and fulfills a vital role.

Nuclear Wasteland
A further reason that small, extended family type churches must multiply in these days is to help fill the devastating void caused by family break-up. Not only has the nuclear family been devastated by divorce and separation but the extended family rarely functions given distances between relatives and the mad pace of life. Last, the

local community, which for centuries was so settled and strong, barely exists in these days of Internet shopping, emails and TV.

More people than ever are living alone and the most human interaction some receive each week is a grunted platitude from a bored checkout girl. More and more young people are becoming absorbed with computer games to provide surrogate friendships and many older folk experience life only through their TV screens. We might say to them, "Come on, get a life," but would their reply be . . .?

Why get a life when you've got a TV?

Why get a life when you've got a TV?
It's my window on the world; I don't need to really "Be."
I've traveled round the globe on this lumpy settee,
So who needs a life when you've got a TV.

Why seek excitement when you've got a TV?
There's a murder every night. In Midsomer there's three!
You may think my life is dull, as I watch predictably,
But why seek excitement when you've got a TV?

Who needs a wife when you've got a TV?
When the world has gone to bed all the girls are there for me.
As I finger my remote, they respond so willingly,
I don't need a woman here; I've got a TV!

Why bother thinking when you've got a TV?
All those soaps will wash my brain from all creativity,
I have all of my opinions delivered here for free.
Who needs to bother thinking when you've got a TV?

Why make friends when you've got a TV?
Wogan, Parkinson and Merton they are always there for me,
They never need my help and we never disagree,
So why make friends when you've got a TV?

Who needs a prison when you've got a TV?
I am locked into the screen by some unseen energy,
For as long as I submit to it I'll never be free,
I don't need a prison, NO! I've got a TV!

Opportunity Knocks

We need to resist the temptation to mope about modern life and the breakdown of the family and instead see it as the best opportunity we'll ever have to reach this lost and lonely generation. Whilst millions are caught in lifestyles of relationship breakdown, social isolation and artificial entertainment, few are content with it. We are made in the image of God, made to find true fulfillment in life-giving relationships with others.

Surely the time has come for the grassroots church. Accepting of all ages and backgrounds, full of grace, based on genuine love and friendship, how can such communities fail to appeal to this broken generation? Conventional church forms will continue to reach some of the marginalized in society, but if we want to see the widespread turning to the Lord that we long for, another reformation is needed. This will not be a reformation of doctrine, but of practice.

For those in peril on the sea

For too long, the central-place church with its smart or imposing building has been like an Ocean Liner sailing through a sea of drowning people who feverishly tread water or grasp onto driftwood. From the high deck, far-off figures shout through megaphones, "Get into the ship, it's safe, it's dry, there's food and shelter!" Some of the drowning people are so intimidated by the size of the boat, they don't even hear the message, and fearing the liner will crush them they swim away. Others listen but are undecided, "We can't see the people in the vessel clearly enough, what if they're lying, perhaps we'll be imprisoned." For a few bold (or desperate) swimmers, they attempt to climb aboard. Grabbing hold of the long dangling ropes they begin a tortuous climb up the vast steel ship. Some get there, but most through exhaustion and discouragement think "I'll never make it" and jump back into the dark, cold waters once more to grab the nearest piece of driftwood.

These three responses mirror the reality of trying to reach a needy world through remote, non-relational methods. People mostly fear the institution so much they don't hear the message. Many others have a listen, but because they do not truly know the people offering the gospel, are unable to discern whether it's true and really works. For the few who are desperate enough to try to join church life the process too often is long winded and uphill and more give up on the way than actually make it through.

What the liner needs to do is deploy the crew into small lifeboats that can row to where the swimmers are. They can talk to them, share their experience with them and answer their questions. Then, they can be hand lifted into the lifeboat, given food and dry clothes.

In time, once the survivors have confidence in their newfound friends, they will be willing, even enthusiastic about meeting others in larger settings from time to time. But perhaps they will always feel most comfortable as part of a life boat crew themselves. . .

If the Hat Fits. . .

However enlightening a sermon may be, it fails if it does not offer practical application. This final section will consider a few situations common to many readers and seek to suggest possible responses.

A) The out of churchers: My heart goes out to the many believers whom the church has failed. Looking back on my own leadership, whilst grateful for the good fruit, I am keenly aware of those for whom I made being part of the church a painful experience. With the benefit of hindsight, I can see that clouded motives made me at times insensitive, at others impatient and sometimes over protective of "my vision" to the point of being controlling or legalistic. In the early years I allowed the expectations of church form to hamper of my real desire, to care and nurture.

If you are a believer who has given up on, or fallen out of church life, I will not insult you with the usual response "You need to be in fellowship." But I dearly wish that something in these pages will have given you some hope that an accepting, friendship based and true-to-life church experience is possible.

Whilst you may be aware of issues in your own life that might have contributed to some of the past difficulties (fear seems the most common, whether of leaders, failure, hurt or rejection), I pray that you will also find grace to forgive those who have let you down.

Augustine once said, so I'm told, "The answer to wrong practice is not non-practice, but right practice." In other words, please don't give up. As a start, can I encourage you to meet up with some Christian friends for a meal and an opportunity to share with and pray for one another? If it leads nowhere else it's a good thing to do anyway and may be a path to healing, but who knows what God might do. Spirit-filled, grassroots churches can spring up in the most unlikely ways.

B) The burnt out brigade: Are you a pastor, elder or small group leader whose passion for God is nearly matched by the toll the church program is taking on your health and family life? I've been there. In 1997 I got so burnt out I must have smelt like a fireplace. Worse still, the frenzied pace created by my expectation of others made us resemble more an overheating boiler than the smooth well oiled machine we were aspiring to be.

There's no one single answer to dealing with stress and too much responsibility, however a mindset change is essential. To recognize that overactivity creates more harm than good. That it is not strong or macho to work too hard, but more often a product of insecurity or lack of wisdom. To be humble enough to recognize that God could do it all without you if he chose, and see that even Jesus could "do nothing by himself; but "only what he sees his Father doing."[6] We also need to realize the work of the kingdom is not done by creating an alternative reality (i.e. a full church program to compete with work, family and community life). But instead, it is to bring the kingdom into all those areas.

The usual advice for under pressure leaders comprises well-intended suggestions like "take a proper day off," "delegate more" and "Build team." Whilst not unwise, the need is so acute for many that such counsel is but a sticking plaster over a gaping wound. Rather than nit picking at leader's diary management, what is needed is a radical pruning of the activities, programs, meetings and initiatives that seem to spring up quicker than weeds in April.

The beauty of the grassroots approach is that you choose to allow an environment to develop where the Holy Spirit ensures that all that you ever wanted from church life—salvation, healing, maturity, mission, strong marriages, good parenting, care for the needy, passionate worship, diverse gifts and social impact—take place naturally. The alternative is what you have now, an array of wobbling plates on sticks that you are dashing around, to give yet another spin in the hope of avoiding the sound of tinkling china. Here are some suggestions—

• Have one good midweek meeting instead of separate prayer meetings, Bible studies and special interest groups.

- Make the midweek meeting all age and at a time when younger families can attend together, try to include a meal.
- Have one good Sunday meeting instead of two.
- Incorporate prayer into those two regular gatherings, rather than feel you must have a special prayer meeting for a few.
- See that working people need most Saturdays and evenings for family and home responsibilities. Evenings are wrong time to be often out; they're God-given for family and rest.
- If you're full time, consider taking the bold step of going part-time. It will give you a healthier balance if you have some different work and help motivate others to get involved.
- See your main role as encouraging and releasing every member in their gifts; create a culture of "one-anothering."

C) **Churches with buildings:** Buildings aren't always bad! It's how we view them and use them that will determine whether they serve us or become an encumbrance. Some helpful principles to pursue:
- Don't call the building the church. Call it a center, a hall, whatever, but please not church. It's only words, but it reinforces the error of centuries that it is the building rather than God and his people that is of central importance.
- Have at least one Sunday a month where the church meets more locally in several homes. (One group could meet in the building so there is someone there for unexpected visitors.)
- Give the building a homely feel. Lay the main meeting room in a circular fashion with lounge style seating and décor.[7]

D) **The bulging home church:** Most churches start in homes and outgrow them. What drew people there in the first place (the buzz, friendliness, informality and sense of team) is quickly lost once the group makes the hitherto usual step of moving out into a hall. A more imaginative and bold approach is to look to "seed" a new home church. This should be done prayerfully, and is not usually best done by halving the group, but allowing a handful of envisioned folk, ideally who live near each other, to meet separately, perhaps alternate weeks at first. This way numerical growth can take place without losing the intimate character of the church. And of course there is still scope for meeting all together in all sorts of ways (monthly celebration, monthly youth night, monthly men's breakfast, monthly ladies' lunch and so on).

It stands to reason that any small gathering taking this courageous path will have to resist those in its ranks who want to go a more organized route. It seems to be human nature to want to control the fluid life of God. It's the Spirit's work to continually be replacing inflexible bottles with supple wineskins in which the ever new wine can be contained and multiplied and then decanted for consumption by a spiritually thirsty world. I'll drink to that.

E) Church planters: The Bible doesn't actually talk about church planting. It does however describe the gospel, and the kingdom, as seed. So whilst we tend to think of starting a new church as a deliberate, organized process—like planting a wood, we can equally expect church emergence to be spontaneous and natural too.

I love to think that there are "churches" —functioning gatherings of believers—that don't yet realize what they are. You see you don't need a group of forty, a full timer and a building to start a church. It could be three devoted friends with open homes and hearts to reach out, surely a wineskin God loves to fill with his best vintage?

The End of the Matter

Few Christians witnessing world events are in much doubt that we are in the end times, and many different opinions about eschatology[8] are on offer (If you don't know what "eschatology" means, it's not the end of the world!). To be simplistic, some say evil is going to get worst and the church will have to survive harsh persecution. Others take an opposite view, that there will be a tremendous revival across the world with millions saved and that things will get better before Jesus returns. Still others argue that both will occur, evil will get worse and God's power greater.

I myself take a pan millennial position (I don't know exactly what will happen, but I'm sure it will pan out all right in the end!). But whatever scenario plays out in reality, I am convinced that God is preparing his Body for both persecution and rapid growth through restoring the small, flexible, unreligious forms that the early church enjoyed and thrived with.

Waxing and Waning

A 1947 prophecy[9] attributed to Smith Wigglesworth, the great Pentecostal evangelist, predicted the charismatic renewal of the 1960s and the new church movement that began in the 1980s. He then predicted a great move of God that would take place "when the new church phase is on the wane." This would begin in Britain, flowing into Europe and on into a final burst of worldwide missionary endeavor. If this is accurate, now is that time as many new church groups disperse, whilst others plateau in their growth.

In a breathtaking episode from 2 Kings chapter 3, Elisha instructs Israel's armies to dig ditches all over an arid plain. Once they have completed this hard task, God responds by filling them with water thus deceiving the Moabite opponents and giving victory to God's people. At times we can feel our culture is spiritually dry, but I am convinced that God is calling us to "dig ditches" with the anticipation that he will fill them. By multiplying groups of devoted disciples, we will be "digging ditches," preparing to contain the deluge of a mighty move of God in which multitudes will be saved, discipled and healed in these end times.

We are living in exciting days. Let us prepare to be fruitful, flexible and mobile, leaving the dry cracked chrysalis of dead structure in our wake as we take to the air on the fresh breeze of the Spirit!

References

[1] *The Lion the Witch and the Wardrobe*, by C.S. Lewis. Copyright C.C. Lewis Estate, 1950.

[2] John 3:20.

[3] Acts 5:41.

[4] Matthew 5:11-12.

[5] 2 Timothy 3:1 and 12.

[6] John 5:19.

[7] We recently visited our friends, Greg and Ruth Haslam at Westminster Chapel. They have a unique problem as hardly any members live in Westminster! Their enlightened response has been to make Sunday a family day with a meal following the morning meeting, in a comfortable, homely lounge in which to rest and fellowship in the afternoon before an early evening prayer time.

[8] Eschatology is the name given to the study of end-times theology.

[9] The full text of this prophecy is readily available on many Internet sites through searching 1947 and Smith Wigglesworth.

Epilogue–One

Life Goes On

"I'm really touched," stammered Mark. His mind raced with ideas of how he could develop the church. He had been earning an income from his small wholesale food delivery business, and it seemed feasible to run that alongside the pastoral work for a while, and then, who knows?

The first few months were very encouraging, the meetings in the village hall drew visitors from the area as word got round. The feeling of teamwork was strong as people pulled together, and numbers grew from 30 to 40 on a typical Sunday.

Of course they had to be a bit more organized. Jackie and Tina headed up the children's work, Jack and Tony became Trustees, and a series of rotas were drawn up to take care of tea and coffee making, chair setting out, greeting and so on. After a few weeks Mark suggested they drop the mid-week meal, mainly as no home could accommodate everyone, and partly because he wanted to do a membership course for the adults on a week night.

Slowly, almost imperceptibly, things changed. The way the chairs were set out was a silent barometer of the shift. In the first meetings at the hall, they had sat in a circle; Phil playing a guitar while Tina sat playing her flute opposite. Now they had an OHP, a small PA system and a fledgling worship band. Two rows of chairs in a semi-circle was the response to this development. But also (and none noticed straight away) a slight formality crept in. There was less sharing, in fact most people seemed to slip into neutral gear as soon as the meeting began. Mark (and Phil when leading worship) would sense the passivity and try to stoke things up, but it was no good—they could not recapture the spontaneity and camaraderie of those early days. The Chairs' response was to re-organize themselves into four slightly curved rows facing the OHP screen and table at the front (No one quite knew what the table was for, but it just seemed proper to have one).

So they settled for a more front led style. Mark (and in time Jack as he became assistant leader) would lead a meeting through and the worship band would select a set of songs in advance. Some of the newcomers (mostly Christians from more traditional churches around about) felt very comfortable with this new church. They were friendly, the music was lively and the preaching helpful and relevant. There was a nice children's group too.

Five years on, Mark and Jackie had a chat on their day off. "You know Mark, it's not the same." They reflected on those early years of unpredictable but delightful fellowship. "God did so much didn't he?" Mark chuckled, "We didn't know what we were doing though!" He'd been full-time for two years now. The church had leveled out to about forty adult members (a handful saved into the church, but most were transfers from other congregations) and ten children. Their generous giving covered his salary and the other church expenses. Mark was very busy with pastoral work, preaching and all the "stuff" that went with being a pastor.

Jackie and Mark chatted some more as they walked the dog along the old railway track, and then fell silent. After a few minutes

Jackie asked, "Do you miss them—the early days I mean?" Mark thought about the week ahead; seven meetings, a pile of letters to reply to (some were weeks overdue), two knotty pastoral issues, and the pressure one of the new couples was putting on him to adopt their view of the end times). "Yeah love, I do miss it?" Jackie probed a bit deeper, "Would you go back to all that. . .organized chaos . . .if you could?" Mark's eyes lit up as he relived the freshness and friendliness which had so inspired him at the beginning and turned to Jackie with a smile, "Like a shot!"

Epilogue–Two

Life Goes On

"I'm really touched," stammered Mark. But there was obviously something else he wanted to say, but clearly it was important as he paused to select his words carefully. Finally he spoke;

"You know this last year or so has been the happiest of my life. I've been in church life since I was a kid, but as hard as I tried to fit in, I've always found it frustrating. Don't misunderstand me, I love God and loved being with his people, but somehow every church I've been to has got bogged down with traditions and formats and to be honest, much of the time it's been a bit of a treadmill.

When we moved here we prayed about what church to go to and visited a few, but it seemed that God didn't direct us anywhere. So we met in our home as a family and. . .well God has done so much. . .without us really trying.

I guess what I'm trying to say is—as nice as the idea of becoming a "proper church" might be—when I look at the New Testament I've come round to thinking that what we have here is far closer to what the early church was like than anything else I've known. I would be devastated to lose it."

The group did not appreciate it at the time, but this was perhaps the most pivotal moment in their history. Instead of going down the well-worn path of becoming an organized church, they gave time to praying and hearing God.

A few weeks later, Tina had a dream about a rhubarb plant being split by a spade, and a hand planting a quarter of the root a few feet away from the original one. Quick to dismiss it as result of her fondue meal the previous evening, she soon forgot about it. Then, one fellowship evening, her dream came back to mind just as someone shared from Acts 13 about Saul and Barnabas being set apart. She felt excited and moved by the Spirit to share it, but not before Lily (who rarely read out Scriptures) brought the verses from Isaiah 54 about "spreading out to the right and to the left."

As Tina tentatively shared the dream, there was an unexpected response from Tony and Jean and a younger couple they had introduced a few months earlier. It was a mixture of laughter and amazement and Mark asked them to explain their reaction. It was Jean who spoke up; "We had a meal together, the four of us, a couple of weeks ago. And we just started talking about how it would be great to have a group like this where we live. We've all got friends we'd love to bring to the Lord. It's just we're not gifted like you and Jackie, and we'd hate to stop meeting with you lot!" Mark said simply, "Well it seems like God is right in it, whatever your objections!" They prayed and talked some more and agreed that—for a few months—the original group would meet at Jack and Tina's while Mark's family traveled the five miles to Newton to help the new group get started. Once a month on a Saturday they'd all meet together for a walk and a sandwich lunch.

The first few weeks were remarkable only for the problems. Illness, disagreements, car trouble, work call-outs and discouragement made it all seem a mistake. But pretty soon, folk got wise to what was happening and prayed more purposefully into the new advance.

After four months, things started to happen and guess what—totally different. One evening, Tony and Steve (the husband of the younger couple) went for a walk after their shared supper and ended up kicking a ball around with some teenagers at the park.

After the game they got talking about God and the lads were disarmingly honest about their fears and problems at home. Steve's wife Sue knew one of the Mums, who was more than happy for her son and his mates to spend some time with "decent people." So the group jumped from six to ten in one week as the lads came round for some grub, a few games of darts and to find out more about God. It was great for Mark's children too, as they had kids of their own age coming, and the teenage lads appreciated Phil's rocky guitar style.

A year on and several of the boys had become Christians and now two of the Mums are visiting the group regularly as a result. Mark and Jackie rarely needed to come across now as Tony and Jean's confidence and faith had grown enormously.

As they walked the dog along the old railway line one Sunday morning, Mark and Jackie thanked God for all he was doing both in the new group and the original one that had also grown again. "I wonder what God's got for us next" Jackie mused. Mark smiled "I've no idea, but I can't wait to find out!"

Biographical Note

Duncan Kellard was born in Poole, Dorset in March 1964 to Pat and Jenny Kellard, both committed believers. He became a Christian in 1969, attending a Free Evangelical Church with his family until the age of seven.

In 1973 the family moved to pastor Bere Regis' Congregational Church. The Renewal Movement had a big impact on the church, which grew from a small group of elderly members to become a thriving community. Duncan was himself baptized in the Holy Spirit when nine years of age at a Post Green camp, and baptized in Wareham River the following year (1974).

He attended Lytchett Minster School from 1975–1980, during which time he was privileged to witness a powerful revival under the leadership of RE teacher Linda Smith. Two years at Poole Grammar for sixth form ensued and during this time he began attending Waterloo Christian Fellowship where youth leaders Phil and Jan Dowding had a strong influence on his life and spiritual experience. It was at this time he received his "life call" (Psalm 82:3-4).

On leaving school and following a year's work experience the opportunity to attend Roffey Place Christian Fellowship arose. Duncan studied there in 1984 and joined the ministry team for a further year traveling with Bob Gordon and Colin Urqhuart and gaining insights into a variety of disparate church forms and backgrounds.

Back home and into the family electronics business in 1986, an interest in church-based ministry grew through involvement in prison visiting, worship music, youth work and evangelism. In 1988 he joined the local CARE Trust group from which a strong commitment to the pro-life movement grew. He also joined the Movement for Christian Democracy, serving on its National Steering Group in 1991/92.

Duncan met Sara, daughter of a Dorset farmer, in 1988 and they married in 1990. Two years later their son, Joshua was born, their daughter Katie arriving in 1999.

Leadership of Stour Valley Community Church followed in 1993, and the church became part of New Frontiers in 1994. Through this association, the church benefited from the friendship and ministry of numerous godly people including Mike and Denise Frisby, Ken and Sue Matthews, Tony and Sue Goodman, Martyn and Gaynor Dunsford and Alun and June Davies. In 1996 Stour Valley Community Church adopted cell principles which, with the emphasis on every member ministry and small group dynamics paved the way for the home church style adopted more recently.

In 2000, a new phase of overseas ministry opened up and has since included short-term work in Uganda, China, Ukraine, Albania, Malaysia and the Philippines. In 2005, the Kellards received a growing sense of call to work overseas, and at the time of writing they are making final preparations to move as a family to Palawan, an island in the Philippines, where they plan to run a small holding to provide a haven for neglected and abused children.

During the years since 2001, Duncan has felt an increasing leading to develop a simpler approach to church life. In 2002 he received a prophetic word that God was about to put him on his own to teach him things for passing on to the wider church. As God moved fellow members of his team on to other church plants, nations and, in the case of great friend and fellow elder Mike Haine, to Glory, it has at times been a lone path.

However, the excitement of discovery and process of learning have been deeply rewarding, with the growing conviction that, in these last days, God is raising up an emergent movement of simple, passionate communities, through whom every community and each people group will be reached with the good news about Jesus Christ.

THANKS

The following people read drafts of the book and offered helpful advice:

Sara Kellard – Thanks for your encouragement and many suggestions as well as giving me the time that was quite necessary to complete the task.

Jenny Kellard – Thanks for your affirmation and for stopping me from being too outrageous!

Josh Kellard – Thanks for egging me on to finish. I look forward to reading your book very soon.

Gillian Drummond – Your eye for details and grammar was invaluable. It enabled me to make less mistakes, sorry I mean fewer mistakes!

Mike Frisby – Thanks for your belief and insightful suggestions resulting in new sections on the poor and apostolic ministry.

Mike Thompson – Thanks for input on grammar and suggestions on places where I was a bit too raw.

Alan Horler – Thanks for giving me hope God could use this book to stir and encourage.